BALTIMORE
Bicentennial Celebration
January - December 1997

COPYRIGHT © 1996 BY LOUIS C. FIELDS

ALL RIGHTS RESERVED.

PUBLISHED IN USA

LIBRARY OF CONGRESS CATALOGING-IN-PUBLICATION DATA

FIELDS, LOUIS C.

BALTIMORE AFRICAN AMERICAN RESOURCE & TOURIST GUIDE

ISBN 0-9655741-0-5   (FIRST EDITION/PBK.)

INCLUDES BIBLIOGRAPHICAL REFERENCES

1. BLACK HISTORY-MARYLAND-GUIDEBOOKS 2. US HISTORY

TABLE OF CONTENTS

Acknowledgments

Mr. Steven Pace, thank you for providing the initial encouragement and financial support to get this project started.

Mayor Kurt L. Schmoke and Commissioner Daniel P. Henson, III, I sincerely appreciate and thank you for enabling this guide to become a reality.

Ms. Leslie Tucker of The Perfect Word, thank you for your endless hours of typing and retyping. You have done a fantastic job.

A very SPECIAL THANK YOU to the following individuals and groups:

To the sisters and brothers who paved the way. Adrienne, Alagra and Ms. Gloria Nicholson and Jay McCullough, and to Ed Rogers, Michael Duncan, Reverend James Stovall, Ray Bennett, Cathy Hughes, Lisa Mitchell, Deborah Sterrett, Dr. Ron Sharp, Louis Diggs, Lynwood Jackson, Dr. Norman Ross, Roger Lyons, Reverend John L. Wright, Robert Steele, Mr. Patrick Fagale, J.D. Howard, Monroe Frederick, Ricardo Robinson, Robert Reyes, Ernest Queen, and Dr. T.J. Bryan.

The Great Blacks in Wax Museum, The Peale Museum, Maryland Historical Society, Enoch Pratt Library, Afro-American Newspapers, Baltimore Times, Baltimore City Life Museum, Coppin State, Morgan State University and Sojourner Douglass College.

Praise God From Whom
All Blessings Flow,
Louis Fields, Publisher

HARAMBEE 1-12
(Let's Pull Together)-
Welcome
Greetings From The Mayor
Commissioner Daniel P. Henson
Baltimore Urban League
Foreword
BAATC

HABARIJANI - 13-19
(What's The News?)
FYI
African-American Attractions Map
AFRAM Festival
Governor Parris N Glendening

UMOJA *(Unity)* **- 20-23**
African-American Heritage Tours

UJIMA *(Responsibility)* **- 24-48**
African-American Attractions
   Historical Sites

KUJICHAGULIA - 49-72
(Self Determination)
Freedom Fighters

NIA *(Purpose)* **- 73-75**
Education

KUUBMA *(Creativity)* **- 76-85**
Maryland Sports

IMANI *(Faith)* **- 86-89**
Churches

UJAMAA *(Co-economics)* **- 90-126**
Business Service Directory
Maryland Tourism Offices
Baltimore City Attractions

KUTO MAJINA - 127-128
(The Legacy)
Bibliography
Lift Every Voice and Sing

Mayor Kurt Schmoke

TO: *"Families & Friends of Baltimore"*

Particularly for African Americans, Baltimore City is increasingly becoming a major destination point for family reunions, conferences, and weekend trips. It's a city steeped in African-American history and culture, whose historic monuments and museums feature famous Black leaders from across the centuries.

Baltimore City is also making great strides as a growing center for African-American owned and operated businesses. Plans are currently under way to create a unique district in the City's downtown area, featuring cultural, business, and other entrepreneurial opportunities for the Black business community.

The expansion of the Baltimore Convention Center also opens up expanded opportunities for African-American sponsored conventions and conferences to be held in the City.

I invite all of you to come and visit Baltimore -- to share in its many cultural opportunities, to be entertained and educated, and to experience the richness of its African-American heritage. It's a city of all ages and cultures, and a place that celebrates the diversity of its people and its neighborhoods. This year, Baltimore will commemorate its Bicentennial, with year-round festivities, reunions, and historic events. We look forward to the opportunity to host you and your family as you explore and experience the excitement of Baltimore.

Sincerely,

Kurt Schmoke
Mayor

Baltimore
THE CITY THAT READS
Kurt L. Schmoke, Mayor

BALTIMORE - WHERE BLACK HERITAGE BEGINS

THE BALTIMORE RENAISSANCE CONTINUES IN SANDTOWN WINCHESTER

Pictured is the Sandtown-Winchester Nursing Center and the Nehemial Homes.

BALTIMORE - WHERE BLACK HERITAGE BEGINS - 4

Message From Housing Commissioner Daniel P. Henson, III

Welcome to Baltimore, a city of diversity and opportunity. Our housing stock is as diverse as our population. Many who visit Baltimore find this diversification and wide rangte of housing opportunities and prices to be extraordinarily well-suited to their home-shopping needs.

Development opportunities also abound in Baltimore, and I am proud of our record of minority participation in every realm of housing; from planning and design to management and construction. A catalyst for this record is Baltimore's changing skyline. More than $1 billion in development is underway along the waterfront bordering the Inner Harbor. Our neighborhood redevelopment, however, is at an equally exciting pace and posture. In Sandtown-Winchester on the west side, we are transforming a previously distressed community into one of home ownership and choice.

Near Johns Hopkins Hospital complex, we are working with the Historic East Baltimore Community Action Coalition (HEBCACO) to eliminate 800 abandoned properties. These two communities are part of our $100 million Empowerment Zone effort. Over $400 million of construction is underway in rebuilding our public housing communities. Here, our public housing contracts going to African-American owned companies have increased from 5% in 1982 to more than 60% today, which fairly represents our city's overall population mix.

My personal philosophy to redevelopment is that *you can do well while you also do good.* In other words, projects that uplift our community can also benefit those who live in or give back to those communities. Emerson once said, "Thought is the seed of action." With that in mind, and as you tour Baltimore City, consider our diverse housing and economic development opportunities.

Baltimore's newest attractions include *(top to bottom)* the Baltimore Convention Center, the Christopher Columbus Center and the Inn at Pier Five, the only African-American hotel in Baltimore.

While visiting Baltimore, take the Metro subway (Upton stop) and shop and dine at Baltimore's AVENUE MARKET located on Historic Pennsylvania Avenue.

Baltimore leaders at AVENUE MARKET ribbon cutting ceremonies. (l-r) Commissioner Danny Henson, Delegate Howard Rawlings, Mayor Kurt L. Schmoke, Lena Boone, Congressman Elijah Cummings, Senator Larry Young and community leaders.

BALTIMORE - WHERE BLACK HERITAGE BEGINS

Baltimore Urban
Orchard Street Church

For over 170 years the Orchard Street Church has been an integral part of Black life in Baltimore. The congregation began in 1825 when a former slave, Truman Pratt, began holding prayer meetings at his home. Pratt handled the affairs of the Orchard Street Church for over forty years.

Cyrus Moore and Basil Hall were Pratt's partners in purchasing the land for the church site. The first structure was built by former slaves in 1839 and the Sunday School was added the following year. By 1879 the church membership had grown to 1,500 members. The congregation included many prominent Black Marylanders including Harry S. Cummings, who in 1890 became Baltimore's first Black city councilman.

In 1882 the church was incorporated under the name of the Metropolitan Methodist Episcopal Church and was acclaimed as the foremost African-American house of worship in Maryland.

The church became a center of activity in community affairs, conducting cultural and benevolent activities. It became a resource and meeting place for local and national organizations.

Orchard Street Church was most likely used as a point of the Underground Railroad, a "safe house" for run-away slaves. The Church coordinated and planned routes of safe passage, provided food and shelter for the brave fugitive slaves on their way to the north and Freedom.

A passageway from the museum leads to a sub-basement level three floors below, revealing an underground cistern and a portion of the

League
UNDERGROUND RAILROAD

Rogers Lyons

underground tunnel. Perhaps, Harriet Tubman went through here as she helped her people on their way to Freedom!

Orchard Street Church played a crucial role in assisting Blacks, providing jobs, temporary housing, medical care, and of course providing the spiritual nourishment and hope that the entire Black populace so desperately needed.

In the early 1900's the Orchard Street Church became active in politics and created economic cooperatives, educational initiatives and developed numerous "quality of life" programs to assist people. In 1906, the church created a hostel to welcome, house and provide guidance to young African-American women arriving in Baltimore.

The building was vacated in 1970 after Orchard Street church had merged with Garrison Boulevard Episcopal Church. The church remained vacant until 1992 when after extensive renovations the site became the headquarters of the Baltimore Urban League under the leadership of its President and CEO, Roger I. Lyons. Since that time, the Baltimore Urban League has continued the work started by Truman Pratt and former slaves one hundred and seventy years earlier.

In 1976, the late Marguerite Campbell led a successful effort to have the site listed on the National Register of Historic Places. Presently the former Sunday School serves as headquarters for the Urban League. Receptions and special events are held at the site on the first floor.

Future plans include the opening of the Orchard Street Church Museum on the second level. The museum will present the inspiring story of the Black Church in Baltimore.

Mr. Lyons spearheads the League's activities which include education and employment services, training on the Internet and using the Information Super Highway, counseling young couples in parenting skills and developing award-winning HIV/AIDS awareness programs. The League is also a certified voter registration center and election polling site.

In 1995, the U.S. Bureau of the Census designated the League as a Census Data Analysis and Dissemination Center. Even the townhouses in the area have been renovated in preparation of the League's expansion plans and programs. Plans include a Parent Resource Center and a Child Care Center, and Urban Environmental Center and the Orchard Street Church Museum.

In 1997, the Baltimore Urban League will celebrate 75 years of advocacy and social service to the Baltimore Community. For a tour call 410-523-8150.

FOREWORD
by Dr. Bettye J. Gardner

It is extremely important that the present generation of African-Americans come to understand and appreciate the rich history which is theirs in Baltimore and throughout the state of Maryland. The writer Paul Marshall has written that you have to "engage the past if you are going to shape a future that reflects you."

In the decades before the Civil War, African-Americans in Baltimore comprised the largest free Black community in the nation, numbering 25,000 by 1860. Believing that what transpired within their community was more important than what happened to it, these African Americans built a multifaceted infrastructure composed of churches, schools, and fraternal and beneficial societies. Based on the Baltimore model, the generations that followed relied on their own resources to pass on to communities throughout the state which continue to this day.

Louis Fields has made a major contribution to our knowledge of the African-American presence in Maryland by compiling this historical account of their contributions.

Dr. Bettye J. Gardner is a Professor of History at Coppin State College. She has taught at Coppin for over 24 years. A native of Vicksburg, Mississippi, Dr. Gardner earned her Bachelor and Masters Degrees in History from Howard University. She received her PH.D in History from George Washington University. Dr. Gardner is the National President of the Association for the Study of African-American Life in History, an organization founded by Dr. Carter G. Woodson in 1915.

THE DEDICATION TO CARTER G. WOODSON (1875-1950)
The "Father" of Negro History

We have a wonderful history behind us...
It reads like the history of people in an heroic age...
If you read the history of Africa, the history of your ancestors — people of whom you should feel proud-you will realize that they have a history that is worthwhile. They have traditions that have a value of which you can boast and upon which you can base a claim for the right to share in the blessings of democracy.
We are going back to that beautiful history and it is going to inspire us to greater achievements.

Dr. Carter G. Woodson

THE BALTIMORE AFRICAN AMERICAN TOURISM COUNCIL, INC.

THE BALTIMORE AFRICAN AMERICAN TOURISM COUNCIL, INC. ("BAATC"), a non-profit organization, was formed in March 1996. The mission of Council includes organizing, promoting and supporting the participation of African American businesses, institutions, and entrepreneurs in Baltimore's Travel and Tourism industry.

Louis C. Fields, Executive Director

As Director of The Council, it is my belief that Baltimore should be a premier destination for Black travelers and conventions. The City of Baltimore and the surrounding counties offer visitors the best of mainstream and cultural attractions.

Come to Charm City and celebrate Baltimore's Bicentennial Birthday in 1997. For an enriching cultural experience visit Baltimore natives Billie Holliday, Thurgood Marshall, Eubie Blake, Reggie Lewis and over 100 (African-American Wax Figures) in the Great Blacks in Wax Museum. Visit Historic Pennsylvania Avenue, the Eubie Black National Museum or stop by the Cab Calloway Jazz Institute.

Heritage tours are easily arranged for large or small groups. Call the Council for African American Points of interest and order your copy of the Baltmore Metropolitan African American Tourist Guide.

For fine dining in the downtown area visit Larry Stewart's Sports Place and the Redwood Grille, both restaurants feature great food, cocktails and live entertainment.

Ready to eat B'MORE style, try La Tesso Tana's Restaurant, Captain Gee's Crabhouse & Seafood Restaurant and Micah's Restaurant. For breakfast try the Yellow Bowl and the Caribbean Kitchen.

For festival goers, come to AFRAM, ARTSCAPE, STONE SOUL PICNIC, DIVERSITY DAY, THE PEOPLE'S EXPO or FOR SISTER'S ONLY.

Charm City awaits you!

BALTIMORE AFRICAN AMERICAN TOURISM COUNCIL, INC.
P.O. Box 3014 ♦ Baltimore, MD 21229
410-783-5469 ♦ 410-566-5254 *(fax)*
1-800-860-1200 ext.960992

UNITED BAPTIST MISSIONARY CONVENTION

Located just one block from Martin Luther King Blvd., the three story building has over 51,000 square feet, offices, a credit union, meeting space and have a full banquet facility on the lower level.

Organized Black Baptist of Maryland had its beginning in 1834 when Reverend Moses Clayton, an ex-slave came to Baltimore to carry on religious work among his people. Clayton initially started a Sunday School movement and by February 20, 1836, he had organized the First Colored People's Baptist Church in Maryland.

By 1882 the first convention among Negroes was established. Dr. Harvey Johnson, then Pastor of Union Baptist, along with Calvary Baptist formed the Colored Baptist Convention in 1897. In 1926 the officers of the Co-operative and the Colored Baptist came together to form the United Baptist Missionary Convention of Maryland.

UBMC is a member of the National Baptist Convention which is the largest organized body of Black Christians in the world (7.3 million members). The National Baptist Convention, USA, INC meets annually the week after the first Lord's day in September.

The Women's Auxiliary of the UBMC was formed in 1926, and three years later the junior department was added.

DR. JOHN L. WRIGHT, PRESIDENT
United Baptist Missionary Convention
& Auxiliaries of Maryland, Inc.
940 W. Madison Street Baltimore, MD 21202
410-523-2950 410-523-0258(fax)

FYI BALTIMORE

Information Hotline	783-5469
Ambulance ♦ Fire ♦ Police	911
Public Transportation (bus, light rail, metro subway)	539-5000
BWI Airport	859-7111
Cabs	323-4222
Amtrak	872-7245
Johns Hopkins Hospital - Wolfe & Monument Sts.	955-9000
Liberty Medical Hospital - Liberty Road	383-4000
Maryland General Hospital - 827 Linden Ave.	225-8100
Mercy Hospital - 301 St. Paul St.	332-9477
University of Maryland Medical Center - 22 S. Greene St.	328-8667

Take MTA to sightsee, and save your money for more important things.

(Museums, baseball, crabs, etc.)

Let MTA take you to all the sights. It's the most convenient and economical way to see the Baltimore/Washington area. So see more and spend less. Call (410) 539-5000.

Maryland Department of Transportation

MTA MASS TRANSIT ADMINISTRATION

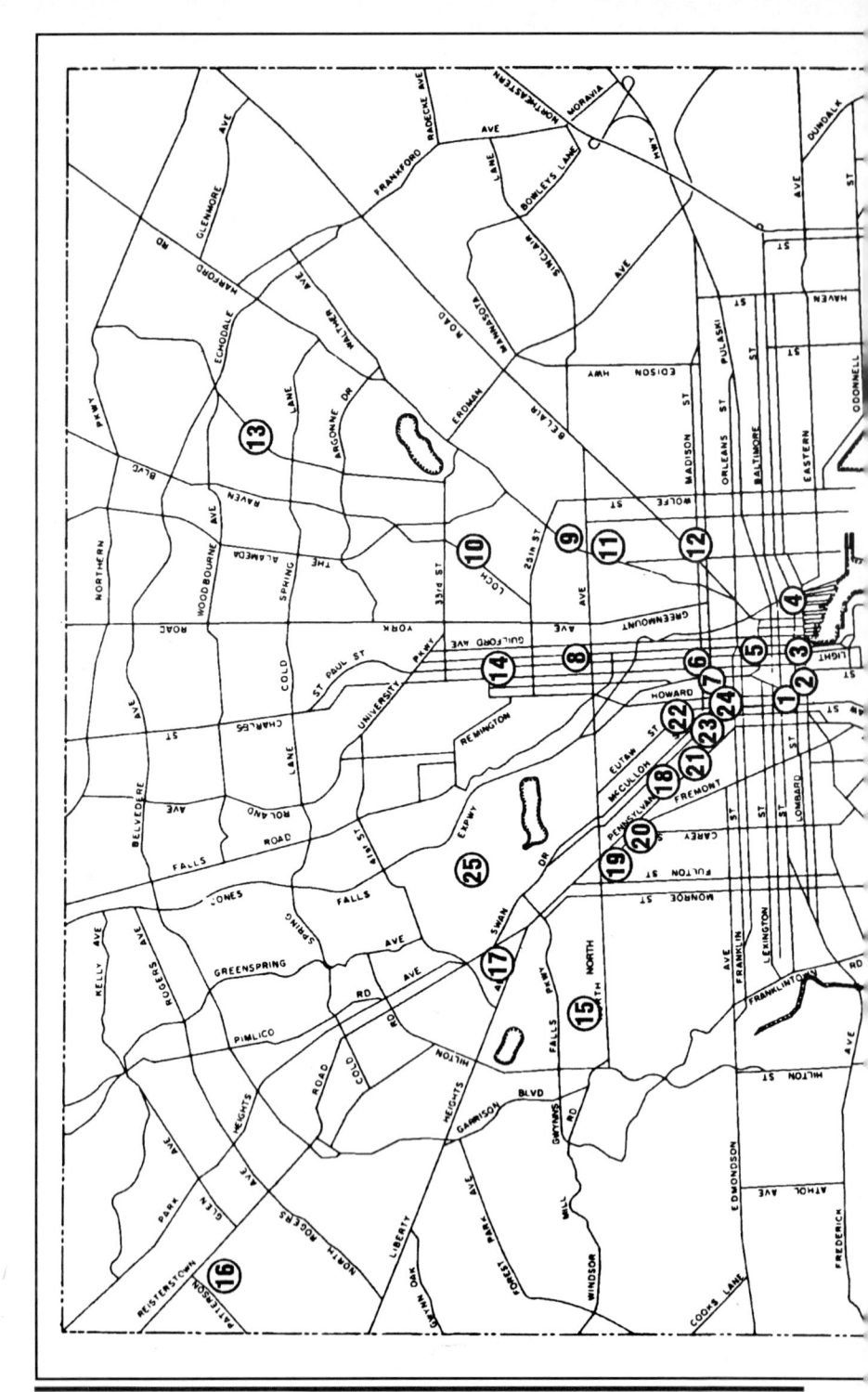

BALTIMORE - WHERE BLACK HERITAGE BEGINS - 14

Baltimore Afro-American Points of Interest

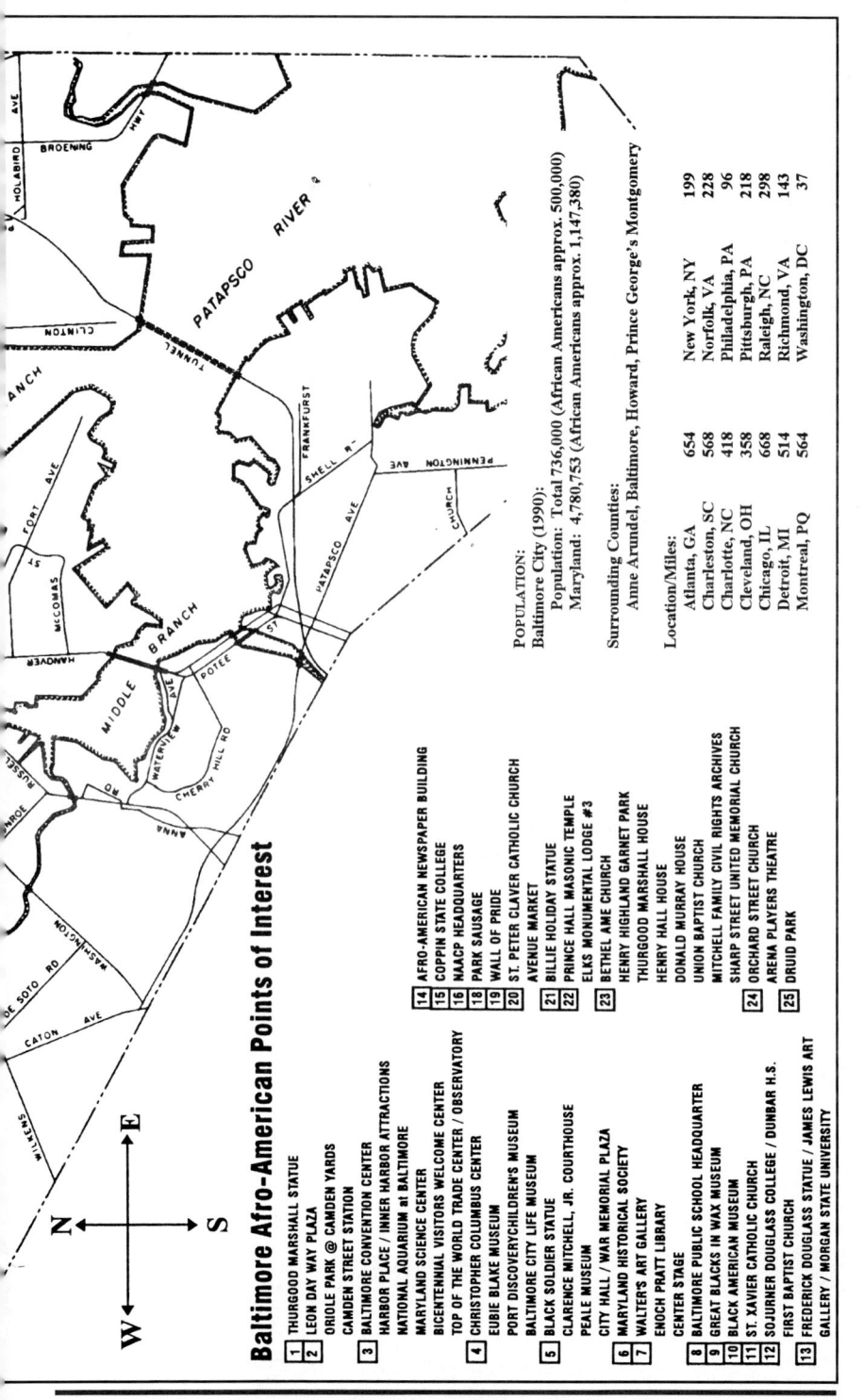

1. THURGOOD MARSHALL STATUE
2. LEON DAY WAY PLAZA
   ORIOLE PARK @ CAMDEN YARDS
   CAMDEN STREET STATION
3. BALTIMORE CONVENTION CENTER
   HARBOR PLACE / INNER HARBOR ATTRACTIONS
   NATIONAL AQUARIUM at BALTIMORE
   MARYLAND SCIENCE CENTER
   BICENTENNIAL VISITORS WELCOME CENTER
   TOP OF THE WORLD TRADE CENTER / OBSERVATORY
4. CHRISTOPHER COLUMBUS CENTER
   EUBIE BLAKE MUSEUM
   PORT DISCOVERY/CHILDREN'S MUSEUM
   BALTIMORE CITY LIFE MUSEUM
5. BLACK SOLDIER STATUE
   CLARENCE MITCHELL, JR. COURTHOUSE
   PEALE MUSEUM
   CITY HALL / WAR MEMORIAL PLAZA
6. MARYLAND HISTORICAL SOCIETY
7. WALTERS ART GALLERY
   ENOCH PRATT LIBRARY
   CENTER STAGE
8. BALTIMORE PUBLIC SCHOOL HEADQUARTER
9. GREAT BLACKS IN WAX MUSEUM
10. BLACK AMERICAN MUSEUM
11. ST. XAVIER CATHOLIC CHURCH
12. SOJOURNER DOUGLASS COLLEGE / DUNBAR H.S.
    FIRST BAPTIST CHURCH
13. FREDERICK DOUGLASS STATUE / JAMES LEWIS ART GALLERY / MORGAN STATE UNIVERSITY
14. AFRO-AMERICAN NEWSPAPER BUILDING
15. COPPIN STATE COLLEGE
16. NAACP HEADQUARTERS
    PARK SAUSAGE
18. WALL OF PRIDE
20. ST. PETER CLAVER CATHOLIC CHURCH
    AVENUE MARKET
21. BILLIE HOLIDAY STATUE
22. PRINCE HALL MASONIC TEMPLE
    ELKS MONUMENTAL LODGE #3
23. BETHEL AME CHURCH
    HENRY HIGHLAND GARNET PARK
    THURGOOD MARSHALL HOUSE
    HENRY HALL HOUSE
    DONALD MURRAY HOUSE
    UNION BAPTIST CHURCH
    MITCHELL FAMILY CIVIL RIGHTS ARCHIVES
    SHARP STREET UNITED MEMORIAL CHURCH
24. ORCHARD STREET CHURCH
    ARENA PLAYERS THEATRE
25. DRUID PARK

POPULATION:
Baltimore City (1990):
Population: Total 736,000 (African Americans approx. 500,000)
Maryland: 4,780,753 (African Americans approx. 1,147,380)

Surrounding Counties:
Anne Arundel, Baltimore, Howard, Prince George's Montgomery

Location/Miles:

Atlanta, GA	654	New York, NY	199
Charleston, SC	568	Norfolk, VA	228
Charlotte, NC	418	Philadelphia, PA	96
Cleveland, OH	358	Pittsburgh, PA	218
Chicago, IL	668	Raleigh, NC	298
Detroit, MI	514	Richmond, VA	143
Montreal, PQ	564	Washington, DC	37

BALTIMORE - WHERE BLACK HERITAGE BEGINS - 15

Special Features

* A Moving and Compelling Exhibit takes visitors below the decks of a 19th century slave ship.

* Exciting Wax Figure Displays
    - And a little Child Shall Lead the Black Youth in the Struggle
    - African Americans and the Christian Faith
    - The great kings and queens of Africa
    - Granville T. Woods (Inventor)

* A Newly Remodeled Gift Shop offering an expanded collection of souvenirs, educational materials and cultural mementos.

A Snack Bar with light refreshments to satisfy your hunger and quench your thirst

Mention This Ad and Receive a 20% Discount
Valid For One Admission Only

The Great Blacks In Wax Museum, Inc.
1601 E. North Avenue ♦ Baltimore, MD 21205
410-563-3404

MARYLAND'S #1 AFRICAN AMERICAN TOURIST ATTRACTION

BALTIMORE - WHERE BLACK HERITAGE BEGINS - 16

THE **AFRAM** LEGEND

AFRAM '97 will take place on September 6-8, 1997 at Oriole Park at Camden Yards. This is the 21st year of celebrating the AFRAM Expo & Festival in Baltimore.

Themes are selected for each festival, such as, AFRAM Salutes the Black Genius, AFRAM Salutes the Black Woman, AFRAM Salutes the Black Family, Black Business, Black Athletes, Black Civil Rights Activities, Black Fraternal Organizations, Black Educators, Blacks in Medicine and The African American Woman. Last year AFRAM Saluted our Public Defenders in Uniform. This year AFRAM saluted our Greater Baltimore African American Communities: "A Portrait of a People in the City by The Bay."

The last two AFRAM Celebrations have included a special appearance by the Negro League Baseball All Stars. During the 1996 AFRAM Festival the first annual AFRAM Sports Heroes Breakfast was held at the Baltimore Marriott Inner Harbor Hotel. The event was organized by Mr. Louis C. Fields.

Louis Fields, Ernest Burke, Eddie Butcher; Sam Lacy Eddie Butcher, Sr. and Lenny Moore

Baltimore

PAST

ALLEY HOUSES

As Blacks migrated to Baltimore during the 1800s, many of them gained employment as domestics in the larger homes of white citizens. Three times before World War I the Baltimore City Council passed laws forbidding Blacks and whites from residing on the same streets. Blacks lived in small houses on narrow "alley streets" located behind major streets in downtown Baltimore, Upton, and Harlem Park.

Alley streets were named Madison, Butler, Morris, Moore, Tripolitis, Tyson, Gillingham, Foster, Stockton, Dawson, Jenkins, Flip, Webster, Indoes, McCellan, Allen, Cohen, Slemmer, Guilford, Hargrove, and Penn Street. By 1910, 23,000 black people lived east of Pennsylvania Avenue amidst 7,500 whites, but west of Pennsylvania Avenue, 8,000 black people lived on alley streets behind all white blocks. Although, most of the Alley Streets were destroyed, streets such as Penn, Stockton, Hargrove and others still exist. *Source: Maryland Historical Magazine & Flower of the Forest by Ms. Eva Slezak*

PRESENT

EMPOWERMENT ZONE (EZ)

On December 21, 1994, President Clinton designated Baltimore as one of six cities to be awarded a $100 million federal grant. Baltimore's Empowerment Zone covers 6.8 square miles. Includes 33 neighborhoods with over 72,000 residents. Already 1600 new jobs have been created in Baltimore's EZ. Baltimore's Empowerment Zone goal is to create self-sustaining communities in West and East Baltimore and Fairfield. Mathias J. DeVito, chair of the Empower Baltimore Management Corporation states "our first priority is to create jobs."

For further information contact:

Baltimore's Business Empowerment Center, 34 Market Place, Suite 801, Baltimore, MD 21202. 410-783-4222.

Empower Baltimore Management Corporation, 111 S. Calvert Street, Suite 1550, Baltimore, MD 21202. 410-783-4400.

STATE OF MARYLAND
OFFICE OF THE GOVERNOR

PARRIS N. GLENDENING
GOVERNOR

ANNAPOLIS OFFICE
STATE HOUSE
100 STATE CIRCLE
ANNAPOLIS, MARYLAND 21401
(410) 974-3901

WASHINGTON OFFICE
SUITE 311
444 NORTH CAPITAL STREET, N.W.
WASHINGTON, D.C. 20001
(202) 638-2215

TDD (410) 333-3098

DEAR FRIENDS:

Maryland has so much to offer -- beautiful countryside, historic towns, bustling cities and an abundance of shorelines boarding on the Chesapeake Bay and the Atlantic Ocean. Maryland also has a reputation for hospitality and I want to extend that hospitality by welcoming you to our State.

Planning a family vacation that focuses on black history is easy in Maryland. Through out the State, you will find a legacy of African-American history and culture. And there are many ways to enjoy that history. In Annapolis, there is an audio walking tour designed to highlight the African-American heritage in that historic city. Baltimore is home to the famous Great Blacks in Wax Museum and the lovingly restored Orchard Street Church. On Maryland's Eastern Shore, visitors can follow portions of the Underground Railroad and visit the birthplace of Harriet Tubman.

In Maryland, you will discover that there are many things to see and do that will help you discover the history and culture of African-Americans. I hope you enjoy your visit to Maryland and come back again soon.

Parris N. Glendening
Governor

A Baltimore African-American HERITAGE TOUR

The African-American Heritage Tour starts at the corner of Pratt and Light Street, the site of Baltimore's Inner Harbor where the first slaves arrived to work the docks of Baltimore-Town. Some Blacks were sold at the slave auction blocks which were located near today's Baltimore Convention Center.

The SHARP STREET MEMORIAL UNITED METHODIST CHURCH (1787) started at the corner of Pratt and Hopkins Plaza close to where a statue honors Baltimore native THURGOOD MARSHALL. Marshall was the first African-American to sit on the United States Supreme Court.

ISAAC MYERS organized a Black owned shipyard, the CHESAPEAKE BAY DRYDOCK & SHIPYARD COMPANY in the harbor of Baltimore.

Other downtown sites of interest to tourists seeking to experience the heritage of Blacks in Baltimore include the Camden Street Station where HARRIET TUBMAN led many slaves including her parents from slavery to freedom.

In 1995 Baltimore Mayor Kurt L. Schmoke renamed the Plaza "THE LEON DAY PLAZA".

Heading east on Pratt Street the renaissance of Baltimore's Inner Harbor includes the Maryland Science Center, Harborplace Pavilions, the World Trade Center and the City's top tourist attraction, the National Aquarium at Baltimore. MR. HENRY HALL, an African-American from Baltimore was one of the first to donate a fish collection (over 10,000 specimens) to the Aquarium.

The President Street B&O Railroad Station is located at President and Fleet Streets. FREDERICK DOUGLASS made his escape from his slave owner's home in Fells Point via this train stop. A new African American Museum will be located near here soon.

From Pratt Street turn left on Calvert Street, there's two African-American restaurants, LARRY STEWART'S SPORTS BAR at 21 S. Calvert and at 12 S. Calvert is the REDWOOD GRILL.

Next stop is Calvert and Lexington Streets where the BLACK SOLDIER STATUE stands to the north side of the Battle Monument. Directly across from the Black Soldier Statue sets the CLARENCE MITCHELL, JR. COURTHOUSE.

AMERICA'S FIRST Black History Wax Museum

Norman & Marie Jones of Columbus, Ohio

Proceeding north on Calvert and turning right onto North Avenue, let's head to Maryland's number one African-American tourist attraction, the GREAT BLACKS IN WAX MUSEUM at 1601 E. North Avenue. For lunch (dinner) try MICAH'S RESTAURANT at 5401 Reisterstown Road or for fine dining seekout LA TESSO TANA'S at 58 W. Biddle Street.

Proceed back (east) up North Avenue past the school headquarters turn left onto North Charles Street to 2509 N. Charles and visit the offices of the BALTIMORE AFRO-AMERICAN NEWSPAPERS. The AFRO was founded in Baltimore (1892) by an ex-slave, John Murphy.

Circle back to North Avenue heading West to 1356 W. North Avenue to EVERYONE'S PLACE CULTURAL CENTER, three floors of Afrocentric merchandise including Kente Cloth, books, clothing, art and more.

Proceeding up North Avenue, turn left onto HISTORIC PENNSYLVANIA AVENUE, next turn right at the first light. Turn left at the next corner and on the left side is the WALL OF PRIDE, an African-American mural.

Circle the block back to HISTORIC PENNSYLVANIA AVENUE and ride through the area where during the 30's, 40's and 50's Black culture flourished. The Avenue was home to over 50 Black owned businesses including markets, ice houses, restaurants, nightclubs and the famous ROYAL THEATER. Black entertainers such as REDD FOXX, BILLIE HOLIDAY, JACKIE "MOMS" MABELY, JAMES BROWN and all the stars of the time, played the famous ROYAL THEATER.

Bill Pickett

At the corner of Pennsylvania Avenue and Fremont Avenue is ST. PETER CLAVER ROMAN CATHOLIC CHURCH (1888), the first parish in the world dedicated to St. Peter Claver known as the "Apostle of the Slaves".

Across the street is the former SPHINX CLUB. From here pass through "LITTLE WILLIE ADAMS" block (the 1500 block of the Avenue).

The LAFAYETTE MARKET has been renovated and has over 20,000 square feet of retail space featuring fresh and prepared foods, ethnic products for sale and gift items.

The next stop is 1601 Pennsylvania Avenue where former Baltimore Colt Glenn Dougherty financed the "SHAKE & BAKE" youth center, today it's named the NEIGHBORHOOD RECREATIONAL CENTER housing a skating rink, a bowling alley and offices for city agencies.

Continuing down HISTORIC PENNSYLVANIA AVENUE to the corner of Lafayette and Pennsylvania Avenue, the statue of BILLIE HOLIDAY is located directly across from Providence Baptist Church. Born in Baltimore on April 7, 1915, BILLIE HOLIDAY was known as the world's greatest jazz singer.

The ROYAL THEATER was once located across the street on the playground of ROBERT C. MARSHALL elementary school.

Turn left onto Lafayette (heading north) go one block turn left onto Division Street, the THURGOOD MARSHALL HOUSE MARKER is at 1632 Division Street. Now, go one block and turn right onto Druid Hill Avenue and stop at the corner of Lafayette and to the left is a park named in honor of HENRY HIGHLAND GARNET.

At the next corner is HISTORIC BETHEL AFRICAN METHODIST EPISCOPAL CHURCH. BETHEL is the oldest independent Black institution in Baltimore, its congregation dates back to 1787.

Proceed to the next light (Dolphin Street) turn left and at the next corner is SHARP STREET MEMORIAL UNITED CHURCH built in 1802. About two blocks to the north at 1353 Eutaw Street is the DR. LILLIE CARROLL JACKSON HOUSE. Also in this block is the headquarters of the PRINCE HALL MASONS and the EASTERN STARS. Also there is a monument honoring Frances Scott Key.

Return to Druid Hill Avenue and cross MARTIN LUTHER KING, JR. BOULEVARD, turn right at Orchard Street and at the first corner is the current home of the BALTIMORE URBAN LEAGUE housed within the HISTORIC ORCHARD STREET CHURCH, a former safe house on the UNDERGROUND RAILROAD.

One block away is the home of the ARENA PLAYERS, America's oldest, continuously operated Black theater. The theater was founded in 1953 by the late SAMUEL WILSON, JR.

Turning right off of Druid Hill Avenue to Eutaw Street, the 104 year old AFRO-AMERICAN NEWSPAPER was located on this corner where the present Landmark apartment building is located.

Heading down Eutaw Street, you'll find several Black owned businesses from the 600 block of Eutaw to the Lexington Market area. **ENJOY**

La Tesso Tana

BALTIMORE'S FINEST RESTAURANT
Cuisine
Italian
American
Seafood
Private Parties
Cocktails

Reservations Are Recommended

Located behind the Meyerhoff Symphony Hall

Chef/Owner ED ROGERS

LaTesso Tana
58 W. Biddle Street ◆ Baltimore, MD 21201

410-837-3630

African-American Attractions and Historical Sites

BALTIMORE:
This has always been a city of milestones for African-Americans. From the days of crusading businessman and labor organizer Isaac Myers, who in 1869 spearheaded the organization of a Black National Labor Union, to December 8, 1982 when newly inaugurated Mayor Kurt Schmoke, created a revolution in reading.

Afro-American Newspaper Headquarters
2509 N. Charles Street, Baltimore, MD 21218, 410-554-8200
104 year old Black newspaper, published weekly on Friday.

African Watering Hole/Baltimore Zoo
Druid Park Lake Drive, Druid Hill Park, Baltimore, MD 21217, 410-366-5466
Six acre picnic area, festivals, sports, including, tennis, swimming, baseball, basketball etc.

Arena Players
801 McCulloh Street, Baltimore, MD 21201, 410-728-6500
Season: September - June The Arena Players, Inc., a Black theatrical group, was founded by Samuel Wilson, Jr.

Baltimore Tennis Marker
Druid Park Lake Drive, Druid Hill Park, Baltimore, MD, 410-396-6136
The marker lists the name of the 24 people arrested in 1948 for protesting Baltimore City's segregated tennis courts.

Banneker Building
14 East Pleasant Street
This was the first office building erected solely for Black professionals. It was dedicated in 1903.

Bethel A.M.E. Church (1785)
1300 Druid Hill Avenue, 410-523-4273
Bethel is the oldest independent Black institution in Baltimore. Its origins date back to the late 18th century. The first pastor, Reverend Daniel Coker, was the author of the first book published by a Maryland Black in 1810 and in 1816 he was elected the first Bishop of the African Methodist Episcopal Church.

African-American Attractions & Historical Sites

Eubie Blake Cultural Arts Center
34 Market Place, The Brokerage, 410-625-3113
>Eubie Blake exhibits is a display of memorabilia and artifacts relating to the life of Eubie Blake from his birth to his 100th birthday.

Black American Museum
1769 Carswell St., 410-276-9600
>This collection consists of Afro-American Art with special emphasis on the period of the Civil Rights movement, Black memorabilia and the art of the Third World.

Black Soldier Statue
Baltimore Monument Plaza, Calvert & Lexington Streets,
>This 9 ft. bronze figure statue by Morgan State University Professor James E. Lewis is dedicated to the memory of the American Black soldiers from all branches of service who served through every American conflict. The statue was dedicated in 1972.

Cab Calloway Jazz Institute
2500 W. North Ave., 410-383-5977
>Coppin State University - Exhibit and memorabilia on the life of Cab Calloway.

Camden Station
333 W. Camden St. @ Eutaw St., Leon Day Way Plaza
>This B&O Railroad station opened in 1857 and Harriet Tubman made it a stop on the infamous Underground Railroad.

Chesapeake Marine Railway and Dry Dock Company
Philpot and Wills Streets
>No longer in existence, this Black-owned enterprise was started shortly after the Civil War when a group of Black businessmen, organized by Isaac Myers, banded together to form this shipyard company in 1866. The company operated a successful business until 1883.

Elks Monumental Lodge #3, 1528 Madison Ave., 383-0826
>The oldest Elks Lodge in operation.

Frederick Douglass High School, Gwynns Falls Pkwy.
>Founded in 1883, this was the first Black public high school in Baltimore.

Frederick Douglass Statue
Morgan State University, Coldspring &Hillen Rd., 410-319-3333
>8-ft. statue designed and sculpted by Professor James E. Lewis.

First Baptist Church
525 N. Caroline Street
>First Baptist, the state's first Black Baptist Church, was founded in 1836, by Moses Clayton an ex-slave, five years after Nat Turner's Rebellion in Virginia.

African-American Attractions & Historical Sites

Birthplace of Joe Gans
Born in 1874, this well-known pugilist won the lightweight crown in 1902 and was the first Black to become a world boxing champion.

Henry Highland Garnet Park
1300 Druid Hill Avenue
Henry Garnet was the son of an enslaved African Chief. He became a Presbyterian Preacher and a lecturer.

Great Blacks In Wax Museum
1601 E. North Avenue, 410-563-3404
America's only Black Wax Museum. Over 100 figures of Africans, African-Americans and others who have played important roles in African-American history. Also features replica of a slave ship.

Frances Ellen Watkins Harper
Harper House, Morgan State University
A popular writer of abolitionist verse, a dedicated teacher and eloquent lecturer. Frances E.W. Harper was born in Baltimore in 1823 and was the first published Black woman novelist in America.

Heritage Museum of Art - Multicultural exhibits
4509 Prospect Circle, 410-664-6711

Billie Holiday Statue
Pennsylvania Ave. between Lanvale & Lafayette, (Billie Holiday Park),
Called "the greatest jazz singer ever, "Billie Holiday was born in Baltimore in 1915.

Dr. Lillie Carroll Jackson Museum
1320 Eutaw Place, 410-523-1208

Joshua Johnson Marker
Morris Mechanic Theatre, Charles & Baltimore Streets
Johnson was the first Black portrait painter whose works won public recognition in the United States. His studio was located near the present Morris Mechanic Theatre from 1796 through the 1820's. A historic marker located there honors him. His paintings hang in the Metropolitan Museum in New York, the National Gallery in Washington, D.C. and the Maryland Historical Society Gallery in Baltimore.

Jackie Lanier Museum
3817 Clifton Avenue, Baltimore, MD 21215, 410-947-5600
Ms. Lanier, a historian and collector has an extensive collection of African-American memorabilia.

Lafayette Square Church
1121 W. Lanvale Street, Baltimore, MD 21217, 410-523-1366
A/k/a Metropolitan United Methodist Church, traces its roots to 1825 under the leadership of Truman Pratt, the founder of Orchard Street Church.

African-American Attractions & Historical Sites

Leadenhall Baptist Church
1021-23 Leadenhall Street, Baltimore, MD
> This church was built in 1873 by the Maryland Baptists Union Association to accommodate the Black Baptist of the Sharp-Leadenhall area.

Leon Day Way
Oriole Park at Camden Yards, Eutaw Street entrance
> Stadium entrance renamed to honor the great pitcher from the Negro Leagues, Leon Day, who became the 12th player from the Negro Leagues to be inducted into the National Baseball Hall of Fame.

James E. Lewis Museum of Art/Parren J. Mitchell Gallery
Morgan State Univ., Sopher Library, Coldspring Ln. & Hillen Rd., Baltimore, MD 21239 ♦ 410-319-3020 ♦ 319-3458, Hours: Mon-Fri 9a.m.-5p.m. African and African-American effects and memorabilia. Weekends call for appointment.

The Liberian Museum of City College
Baltimore City College, 3220 The Alameda, By appointment only.
Tour includes a slide presentation of life in Liberia. (410) 396-7357
> The collection includes such artifacts as utensils, cutlery, instruments, and clothing donated by the citizens and government of Liberia, Baltimore's sister city in Africa.

Thurgood Marshall Bust - University of Baltimore Law Library
Mt. Royal at Oliver Street..

Thurgood Marshall Birthplace
1632 Division Street
> Born and raised in Baltimore, Marshall lived in this house as a young boy. He was denied admission to the University of Maryland Law School because of his race. He attended Howard University, graduating in 1933. In 1967, he became the first Black to sit on the Supreme Court.

Thurgood Marshall Statue, Pratt & Sharp Street

Masonic Temple Prince Hall - Grand Master Sam Daniels
1305 Eutaw Street, Baltimore, MD 21217

Clarence Mitchell Jr. Courthouse
Calvert & Lexington St.
> Courthouse covering entire city block named after the great civil rights advocate.

Mount Auburn Cemetery
> Mt. Auburn Cemetery is the oldest Black cemetery in Baltimore City. Former slaves who found freedom through the Underground Railroad are among the thousands of persons buried there. Mt. Auburn was founded in

1872 by the Reverend James Peck, Pastor, and the Trustees of the Sharp Street Memorial United Methodist Church.

In 1871 the Trustees of Sharp Street purchased land in the Westport community of Mt. Winans. In 1872 the burial ground was officially dedicated and named "The City of the Dead for Colored People." In the years that followed, the name of the property was changed to Mt. Auburn Cemetery, and it became one of the most profitable and humanitarian causes in the ministry of Sharp Street Church.

Joseph Gans, the first Black light heavyweight boxing champion is buried there, as is Dr. Lillie Mae Carroll Jackson, civil rights activist. William Ashbie Hawkins, the first Black man to run for the United States Senate, is interred in Mt. Auburn, as are John Henry Murphy, founder of the Afro-American Newspapers, and many, many other persons from all walks of life.

On December 12, 1986, Mt. Auburn Cemetery was designated a Baltimore City Historic Landmark. A restoration is underway. To support call 410-783-5469.

NAACP Headquarters, National Civil Rights Archives
4805 Mt. Hope Drive, Baltimore, MD 21215, 410-358-8900

Orchard Street Church
516 Orchard Street, 410-528-1850
> Founded in 1825 by Truman Pratt, a former slave of John Eager Howard, this is the 3rd church that has been erected for the congregation at this site.

Parks Sausage
3300 Henry Parks Circle, Baltimore, MD 21217, 410-664-5050
> Home of the world famous "More Parks Sausage, Mom." Parks Sausage was the largest Black-owned manufacturing company in the United States.

Provident Hospital (now Liberty Medical Ctr.)
1600 Liberty Heights Avenue, 383-4029
> The original Provident Hospital was founded in 1894 to provide medical care to Blacks migrating into northern industrial cities, to establish a nursing school for Black women, and to offer training opportunities to Black physicians. The hospital has been moved from its original site and the name changed to Liberty Medical Systems.

Royal Theatre
1329 Pennsylvania Avenue
> In February 1922 the Douglass Theatre opened on this site billing itself as the "finest colored theatre in America owned and controlled by colored people." The original theatre was demolished in 1971 and replaced by the Robert C. Marshall Elementary School.

St. Francis Academy
301 E. Chase Street
> The original St. Frances Academy was founded in 1828 by a Haitian refugee, Elizabeth Lange, and a Suplician priest, Father Nicholas Joubert. It is the oldest school for Blacks in Maryland. The name has been changed to the Father Charles Hall High School.

St. Francis Xavier Catholic Church(1864)
Caroline & Oliver Streets
> This is the oldest Black Catholic Church in the United States. Father Charles Uncles, founder of the Josephite Order, was ordained there. The original site of the church was Calvert and Pleasant Streets. In 1933 it moved to Caroline and Oliver Streets. In 1870, St. Frances Xavier started the first gospel choir in the archdiocese.

St. Peter Claver Roman Catholic Church
1546 N. Fremont Avenue, Baltimore, MD
> (1888) Founded by the Josephite Fathers, this was the first parish in the world dedicated to St. Peter Claver, the "Apostle for the Slaves."

Sharp Street United Methodist Church
Dolphin and Etting Streets
> (1802) Sharp Street Church descends from the first Black congregation in Baltimore.

Union Baptist Church
1219 Druid Hill Avenue
> Organized by John Carey in 1852, the church became a center for the civil rights struggle.

Wall of Pride
Carey & Cumberland Street,
A Mural Portraying Black Leaders.

Eubie Blake

National Jazz Museum & Cultural Center

The Eubie Blake National Jazz Museum & Cultural Center had its roots 25 years ago in the Model Cities Cultural Arts Program. The program was initially designed by Model Cities to provide leisure and recreation activities for inner city youth. However, it took on an educational aspect and became a serious entity in the lives of many inner city people. The Cultural Arts Program provided opportunities for people to learn the arts, discover hidden or innate talents and visit places they never had the privilege of visiting before. Activities offered included summer workshops which provided opportunities for participants to work with nationally known artists in dance, theater, music and photography. Some of them were Eleo Pomare, Ossie Davis and Ruby Dee, Jimmy Heath, Chuck Davis, Rod Rodgers, Katherine Dunham and others. In December 1983, the Center was made part of the Urban Services Agency.

In 1984, the estate of Eubie Blake approached the City about leaving his archives. As a result of his gift, the Center was renamed the Eubie Blake National Museum & Cultural Center. A permanent exhibit to chronicle his life was installed at the Charles Street location. In 1993, a fire burned down the Center and a search began for a new location.

In 1994, the Eubie Blake National Jazz Museum and Cultural Center became a private non-profit corporation with 501(c)(3) status. In 1995, the Howard Street location was identified and work began towards creating a new home for the Center. Presently, the museum is located in the Brokerage at 34 Market Place.

The new site is a corner location on Franklin and Howard Street with approximately 20,000 square feet of exhibit space. The Eubie Blake Jazz Center will be one of many tourists attractions on Howard Street "Avenue of the Arts." Mr. Leslie Howard succeeded Dr. Norman Ross as the new Executive Director in 1996.

Ms. Camay Murphy is chairing the fundraising committee to relocate the Eubie Blake Center on Howard Street. Please contact 410-625-3113 to support this worthy cause.

ARENA PLAYERS, INC.

Founded in 1953

Baltimore's Arena Players, Inc. is celebrating its 43rd Season of dramatic productions. It is the nation's oldest continually performing and historically Black community theatre. This has been accomplished over the years through the efforts of a dedicated group of members and a supportive city and government. From its humble beginnings in 1953 by a small aspiring group of ambitious fledgling actors, the Arena Players, Inc. is now a Baltimore institution with a proud history of community service and outstanding dramatic achievements.

SAM WILSON
FOUNDER OF ARENA PLAYERS, INC.

Many of Baltimore's dignitaries and citizens turned out on September 9, 1995, to pay tribute to the late Samuel H. Wilson, Jr. when the 800 block of McCulloh Street was renamed in his honor. Friends, curious onlookers and family were delighted when Congressman Kweisi Mfume unveiled the new street sign bearing the name of the founder and artistic director of the Arena Players, Inc. Samuel Wilson graduated from Coppin Teachers College. He received an M.Ed. in children's literature form Boston University and did graduate work at Trenton State College, Johns Hopkins University, Temple University and the University of Pennsylvania.

Samuel Wilson came back to Coppin in 1971 as an Assistant Professor in the Department of Languages, Literature and Journalism where he remained until his retirement in 1994. Sam made his name in Baltimore when he organized a group of his friends and founded the Arena Players, Inc. in 1953. Sam directed, and performed in plays until two weeks before his death in February 1995.

801 McCullough Street • 410-728-6500

AFRICAN-AMERICAN ATTRACTIONS & HISTORICAL SITES

Beyond BALTIMORE

ALLEGANY COUNTY

African Methodist Episcopal Church, Frostburg, MD
This church was built in 1881 for a total of $800.00. It was the first Black church in the county.

Ebenezer Baptist Church, Cumberland, MD
Along with Carver High School, this church was the site of one of the first schools for Blacks in the county.

Sumter Cemetery, Cumberland, MD
This cemetery contains the graves of Black civil war soldiers

Carver High School
This Black high school originally educated students from Maryland, Pennsylvania and West Virginia.

ANNE ARUNDEL COUNTY

Aris T. Allen Statue, Rte. 665 East, Annapolis, MD

Annapolis City Council, Annapolis, MD
The first Black to be elected to the city council was William H. Butler in 1893.

Highland Beach Community, South of Annapolis
Charles Douglass, son of the famous freedom fighter Frederick Douglass, bought 40 acres of beach front land in response to the racial segregation he and his wife Laura experienced at the Bay Ridge resort outside of Annapolis. Plans were developed for a private, Black community that would be a summer retreat for friends and family. The area became Highland Beach in 1893 and Charles built the first house in 1894. The area was later nicknamed "The Beach" and was so tuned into Black culture that even the streets were named after famous Black people. In 1922, Highland Beach became the second town in the county to become incorporated.

Banneker-Douglass Museum
84 Franklin Street, Annapolis, MD 21401, 410-974-2893
Maryland's official repository of African-American heritage named after two eminent Marylanders, the museum was dedicated on February 24, 1984. Located on Church Circle in Annapolis. The Museum is housed in old Mount Moriah Church. It is listed on the National Register of historic Places.

African-American Attractions & Historical Sites

Brewer Hill Cemetery
Oldest Black owned cemetery in Annapolis.

Kunte Kinte Commemorative Plaque
on Annapolis City Dock, 410-268 TOUR
A bronze plaque commemorates where Kunte Kinte arrived in this country in 1767. Kunte Kinte was an ancestor of Alex Haley as portrayed in his best selling book, Roots.

Martin Luther King, Jr. Tree,
Maryland State House, Annapolis, MD

Matthew Henson Memorial, Maryland State House, Annapolis, MD
A plaque honoring Henson, (a native of Charles County, Maryland) as the first man to reach the North Pole.

Thurgood Marshall Memorial Statue, Lawyers' Mall, Annapolis, MD

BALTIMORE COUNTY

ARBUTUS MEMORIAL PARK
Surrounded by the tiny Black Community known as Cowtown, Arbutus opened in 1936 to "coloreds" who wanted the finest in perpetual care for their loved ones but couldn't be entered into white cemeteries.

> Lillie Carroll Jackson - Civil Rights Leader
> Emerson Julian - Physician & Politician
> Coach Talmadge Hill - Morgan State Univ.
> Henry Parks - Parks Sausage (founder)
> Rev. Theodore Jackson - Gillis Memorial Church
> William "Box" Harris
> Tiffany Smith - Killed at age six by a stray bullet.
> Chick Webb - Jazz Drummer/Discover of Ella Fitzgerald
> Wiley Daniels - Newscaster
> Leon Day - Negro League Baseball Player/Hall of Fame Inductee 1995
> Benjamin Taylor - Negro League Baseball Player
> Al Sanders - TV Newscaster
> Maryland State Senator Troy Brailey
> Alex Schmoke, brother of Mayor Kurt L. Schmoke
> Phyllis Wallace, First African-American Female Professor at MIT

Banneker Marker
Westchester Ave. at Westchester School, Baltimore, MD
This marker is a tribute to Benjamin Banneker, the Black mathematician, astronomer and inventor, who in 1792 produced an almanac regarded as one of the most reliable of its day.

CATONSVILLE: One of Maryland's oldest communities, Catonsville is located just eight miles west of downtown Baltimore. Nearing its 100th Birthday, this area was first settled by the "colored" property owners who

African-American Attractions & Historical Sites

purchased land along Winters Lane. Winters Lane crosses Frederick Avenue south of the area where Benjamin Banneker lived.

EAST TOWSON: This 135 year old Black Neighborhood was settled before the Civil War by Freed Slaves from the nearby Hampton Mansion Estate which was owned by the Ridgelys. It was the first community established in Baltimore County. Hampton House is listed on the National Register of Historic Place. It is located on York Road in Towson near 695 Beltway Exit.

HAMPTON NATIONAL HISTORIC SITE
535 Hampton Lane
Towson, Maryland 21286

African Americans and Slavery: In 1829 there were 155 slaves at the Hampton Plantation. The third master, John Ridgley, purchased new slaves and he owned almost as many slaves as his father had.

Mt. Calvary AME Church (1890)
In 1986 Rev. Ann Farrar-Lightner became the first female Pastor in this Church's history. Four years later, Rev. Lightner became the first woman in 175 years to deliver the opening sermon for the Baltimore Annual Conference of AME Pastors. Also in 1990 she was selected the first female President of the Baltimore and Vicinity AME Ministerial Alliance.

Mt. Gilboa AME Church
Westchester & Oella, MD 21043, 410-465-1700

The Benjamin Banneker Obelisk is located on the grounds of the historic Mt. Gilboa AME Church where Banneker worshipped, attended school and was laid to rest.

The Meeting House, White Marsh, MD
The Meeting House was a social club house for Blacks in the 1850's.

Birthplace of Amanda Smith, Long Green, MD
Amanda Smith was an internationally known evangelist, and a self-educated woman whose knowledge and abilities were admired by scholars and religious leaders throughout the world.

Oblate House, 701 Gun Road, Catonsville, MD
Home of the Oblate Sisters of Providence, the oldest Order of Black Nuns in the country.

Calvert County

Ben's Creek Community
This freed slave community was located near the village of Island Creek and was considered "one of the most progressive and thriving villages around." Today, it resembles a ghost town of abandoned houses and fields. Originally, there were nineteen houses, sixteen of which were log houses. In 1977 four of the houses were still standing along with the log ruins of three others.

Benjamin Foote House, Lusby, MD
This was an original slave cabin on the Thomas R. Tongue plantation. In 1890, this tract of land was sold to Benjamin Foote whose descendants continue to live in the house.

Brooks Administrative Center, Frederick, MD
This building, which currently houses the Board of Education, was named after William Sampson Brooks. From 1939 until 1975, the building served as a school. Until the mid-'60s only Black students attended this school. Brooks, born in Lower Marlboro in 1865 served as a minister in Minneapolis, Chicago, Des Moines, Nashville, St. Louis, Wichita and Baltimore.

Log Schoolhouse, St. Leonard, MD
This one room schoolhouse was constructed of V-notched logs. It was constructed before 1882 and was last used as a schoolhouse in the 1930's when it served the Black community in the area.

St. Peter's United Methodist Church, Chaney, MD
The original church was built in 1857 and has served a small but steady Black congregation typical of rural Maryland.

Holt Whittington House, Dunkirk, MD
This sturdy 1½ story frame house was probably built in the second quarter of the 19th century, to be used as a slave, tenant or small landowner's dwelling. Since 1892, the land has been owned by succeeding generations of the Holts and Whittingtons, local Black families.

Old St. Edmunds United Methodist Church, Sunderland, MD
Originally built of log around 1860, this church also served as a school for Blacks. There have been three churches on this site, the last being destroyed by fire in 1975.

Plum Point School, Willows, MD
This one-room frame building was originally a school for Black children. Before the 1930s, when it was moved to its present location, it was used as a tenant house.

Plank House, Dares Beach, MD
This building resembles the slaves' cabins of the 19th century. Yet, since it is slightly larger and more refined, it was likely inhabited by free Blacks.

Collin Williams Slave/Tenant House, Prince Frederick, MD
Now in ruins, this one-room hewn frame cottage with an attached kitchen may have originated as a slave cabin, it was later used by Black tenants.

Undertaker's Parlor, Prince Frederick, MD
This simple 14'x20' building served as an undertaker's parlor. It was operated by Richard Wilson Mason and served the Black community in this rural area during the second quarter of the 20th century.

Joseph Smith Log House, Prince Frederick, MD
Joseph Smith, a Black farmer, built this two-story, three-bay gable-roofed building before 1908. Covered by two layers of weather boards, the house is constructed of notched logs which were felled on the property.

Rice House, Port Republic, MD
According to local oral tradition, this modest two-story frame house was built as the residence of John Rice, a Black blacksmith.

Alice Rice House, Port Republic, MD
In 1876, Thomas G. Ireland, a prominent planter, sold this tract of land to George W. and Sarah Jane Rice, a Black couple.

Gray House, Port Republic, MD
This house was built by John A. Gray and his son Thomas, at the turn of the 20th century. It is one of the largest houses owned and built by a Black family in Southern Maryland.

Ireland-Mills-Gantt House, Mutual, MD
This 1 1/2 story frame house was built in the late 19th century as a residence for the Ireland and Mills family. Albert Gantt, a slave coachman, frequently drove his owner, Dr. John Parker, here to visit. Gantt served in the Union Army and returned to Calvert County after he was wounded. After several years of farming, Gantt was financially able to purchase the house.

CAROLINE COUNTY

At some point both Frederick Douglass and Harriet Tubman lived in Caroline County.

The Bureau
Located six miles south of Denton, Maryland, off Maryland Route 16. The Bureau was a two story church-like frame building that was built around 1866 to house Eastern Shore activities of the Freedman's

African-American Attractions & Historical Sites

Bureau. The bureau, a federal agency, gave employment and educational guidance to ex-slaves after the civil war. This building was destroyed by fire in the late 1940's.

Patty Cannon House, Reliance, MD
This house was a slave trader house. It is located on the border of Caroline, Dorchester and Sussex County, Delaware. Here Patty Cannon and her gang kept slaves they had captured to sell in the south. The house was rebuilt in 1885 and is today a private residence.

Ridgely Colored School, Chicken Brand Road, Ridgely, MD
This is the only remaining original Black school in the county, as the others have been torn down. Land was donated for the school in 1865. The building has been renovated many times, and until recently served as the Caroline Development Center.

CARROLL COUNTY

Black Sunday School, Keysville, MD
Although not documented, tradition has it that Francis Scott Key started the first Sunday School for Black children in America in Keysville.

Robert Moton Elementary and Robert Moton High School, Westminster, MD
These were the only public schools for Blacks in Carroll County during Maryland's "separate but equal" attitude toward education. Robert Moton Elementary still exists today.

CECIL COUNTY

Sarah Fernandes
Birthplace of Sarah Fernandes (1863), Sarah founded the first neighborhood settlement for Blacks in the United States. She was the first Black Social Worker in Maryland.

Greenhill Plantation/Slave Quarters - Built around 1780
Route 7 West of North East, MD

St. Stephens Episcopal Church
Route 282, 3 miles west of Cecilton at Intersection of Glebe Road
The first Negro minister south of Mason-Dixon was ordained here in 1834.

CHARLES COUNTY

Afro-American Heritage Museum
LaPlata, MD 301-843-0371 for appointment
The museum has information and artifacts of Indian life, home and school; the community life of early colonists, and slavery. There is also a large collection of materials about Matthew Henson and Josiah Henson.

Birthplace of Matthew Henson
Charles County, MD
> The exact location of Henson's birthplace is not documented, but it is known that he was born on August 8, 1866 in the county. He accompanied Robert E. Peary on most of his expeditions, including that to the North Pole in 1909. He was the first Black to reach the North Pole on April 6, 1909.

Camp Stanton, Benedict, MD
> This camp was established in 1863 for the purpose of recruiting and training a Black Infantry during the Civil War. The 7th, 9th, 19th and 30th Colored Infantries were formed and trained here. The first Battle Hymn of Black soldiers recorded during the Civil War era was "They Look Like Men of War", which originated among the men of the Ninth U.S. Regiment encamped at Benedict, MD during the winter of 1863-1864.

Pope's Creek Land, Grant Pope's Creek, MD
> The first Blacks in Charles County were said to have been imported in the 18th Century by Francis Pope, whose land grant on the Potomac River included this area.

St. Matthews United Methodist Church, Newtown, MD
> St. Matthews African Methodist Episcopal Church was established in 1889. It was founded because there was not a Methodist Church for worshipers in this part of the county. The present dining hall at St. Matthews was once the elementary school for the Black children in Newtown.

DORCHESTER COUNTY

Bethel AME Church
> Purchased in 1847. In 1879, Rev. Grenage and early members of Bethel tore down the wooden structure and erected in its place a brick structure which is one of the most beautiful churches in Cambridge.

Brazell Methodist Episcopal Church (1876)
> Located in Bucktown it is the site where the local African-American community has gathered for worship services since slavery days.

Harriet Tubman's Birthplace and Historical Marker
Stanley Institute, Harriet Tubman Coalition, Inc.
P.O. Box 1164, Cambridge, MD 21613, 410-228-0401
> The marker is located at the former site of the Broadas plantation in Bucktown, Maryland - the birthplace of Harriet Ross Tubman.

Harriet Tubman Park
> Located in Cambridge, Maryland, it is the former site of the First African-American county high school. It was burned to the ground

during the 1967 riots following an incendiary speech by civil rights activist H. Rap Brown.

Scenic Long Wharf
Harriet arrived by boat during one of her missions to rescue her sister who was being auctioned at the courthouse doorsteps a few blocks away on historic High Street.

Stanley Institute
Formerly the Rock School founded in 1865. It was the first community school in Dorchester county and one of Maryland's first African-American community schools. Today it serves as the only African-American museum of its kind of Maryland's Eastern Shore.

Waugh United Methodist Church
One of the oldest African-American churches on the Eastern Shore, founded during slavery in 1826.

FREDERICK COUNTY

Dependence by the area's earliest settlers on slave labor in agriculture and industry was an important factor in the development of both city and county up until the time of the civil war. Slaves of unmixed genetic heritage with ironmaking skills designed and then labored in manufactories such as Catoctin Furnace, turning out products for home, farm and government, including Revolutionary War cannonballs. (reprint from the City of Frederick 250th anniversary brochure, 1995)

Asbury United Methodist Church
West All Saints & Court Streets, Frederick, MD
One of the oldest congregations in the city, Old Hill Church was first built in 1818 on the corner of East All Saints Street. Originally a predominantly white congregation, the Black congregation came into full possession of the church in 1864 and in 1870 changed the name to Asbury Methodist Episcopal Church. The site of the present church was purchased in 1912, and the building was dedicated by Bishop William McDowell upon completion in 1921, on the corner of West All Saints Street.

First Missionary Baptist Church, 106 E. 3rd Street, Frederick, MD
Built in 1773 from locally quarried limestone, with 14" thick walls, the first church's congregation was white. The edifice was given to the Blacks of the community in 1863.

BARTONSVILLE - This town was founded by Greenberg Barton, an ex-slave, prior to 1865. Off of 70 East, between Frederick and New Market, there are two Black churches still in use, Mt. Jackson United Methodist and St. James AME.

CATOCTIN FURNACE-CATOCTIN - This 1770s era iron furnace was built by Black slaves, directly from Africa, who were skilled metal workers. An unmarked slave cemetery was uncovered when U.S. 15 was widened. The old stone smelter has been restored and is an interesting landmark.

CENTERVILLE - This area is located on the Route 80 & I-270 corridor. The old Ebenezer United Methodist Church is still in use.

GREENVILLE - This Black settlement, east of Route 80 & 85 was founded after slavery near the base of Sugar Loaf Mountain. A one-room Black school house near the old Forest Grove United Methodist Church still exists.

LICKSVILLE - This Black settlement is located at the Junction of Route 80 & 85 near Point of Rocks. The old Washington Inn in Licksville was used as a slave auction and slave transportation point.

QUINN CHAPEL AME, 106 E. 3rd Street, Frederick, MD
Built in 1835, the first structure also housed the earliest Black elementary school. The original building which was constructed from logs was destroyed.

ROSS-MATHIAS MANSION - SLAVE QUARTERS
114 W. 2nd Street, Frederick, MD
The slave quarters are located behind the Ross-Mathias mansion and was built in 1817 by Colonel McPherson. Also of interest are the original smoke house, ice house, carriage house, and stables. Today, the slave quarters area is an art gallery.

SLAVE QUARTER, TANEY HOUSE
121 S. Benty Street, Frederick, MD
These were the living quarters for the slaves of Chief Justice Roger B. Taney (c.1799) and are complete with work areas for spinning, cooking, and other household tasks.

OTHER POINTS OF INTEREST IN FREDERICK:
The Steener House, Bishop Clagget Center and the communities of New London, Hopeland, Flint Hill, Baker Valley and Sunnyside.

GARRETT COUNTY

Negro Mountain
This historic site honors, Nemesis, a slave who was the first person killed in an Indian battle on this mountain. Follow 70 west from Hagerstown, Negro Mountain is approximately 10 miles south of Cumberland.

HARFORD COUNTY

Birthplace of Ira Aldridge, Bel Air, MD
Born in 1807 in Bel Air, Mr. Aldridge was a famous Shakesperean actor who performed all over Europe and was the first Black to be knighted.

African-American Attractions & Historical Sites

Hosanna School, Hosanna Ave., Castleton Road, Darlington, MD
Established in 1867 by the Freedman's Bureau to assist newly freed slaves. The school was used to educate Black students from 1867 to 1947. It is located next to Hosanna AME Church. Route 1 North near Conowingo Dam.

McComas Institute, Singer Road, Abingdon, MD
Built in 1867 from funds provided by the Freedman's Bureau, the McComas Institute was built for the purpose of educating the African-American citizens of Harford County. It is listed on the National Registry of Historic Places and is also on the list of Historic Landmarks in Harford County. Call: 410-877-9618 or 879-1217

HOWARD COUNTY

Cultural Gallery of Fine Art, Inc.
7262 Cradle Rock Way, Columbia, MD 21045, 410-381-1199

Ellicott City Colored School
Rogers & Main Street, Ellicott City, MD
One of the most notable Black schools in the county.

Howard County Center of African-American Culture
5434 Vantage Point Road, Oakland Manor, Columbia, MD 21045
410-997-3685
Howard County Black History and Artifacts

Log Cabin - Frederick Rd. near Ellicott Mills Dr.
A settler's hut built in 1780, served as a meeting place for members of the St. Luke A.M.E. Church. Relocated & restored.

Maryland Museum of African Art
5430 Vantage Point Road, Columbia, MD 21044, 410-730-7105
Exhibits display a variety of traditional items from African societies.

Nixon's Farm
2800 Route 32, West Friendship, MD 21794, 410-442-2151/800-942-4509
168 acre working farm and event facility specializing in catering large and small groups.

Mt. Pisgah A.M.E. Church, 8651 Old Annapolis Road, Columbia, MD
One of the older Black churches in Howard County.

Harriet Tubman Junior-Senior High
Freetown and Guilford Road, Columbia, MD
This is the last standing segregated high school in Howard County. It operated from 1949 to 1966. A part of a bygone era, it now serves as offices for the Grass Roots Crisis Hotline and Shelter, Citizens Against Spousal Assault and several other community groups.

African-American Attractions & Historical Sites

KENT COUNTY

Black Settlements - Georgetown and Quaker Neck, MD
These two areas in the county are cited in The State of Maryland Historical Atlas as early Black settlements. However, most Black men and women lived as slaves on the property of their owners.

Birthplace of Henry Highland Garnett
An ex-slave, Garnett became a Pastor and anointed orator. He was named Minister to Liberia in June 1881.

Garnett Elementary School
320 Calvert Street, Chestertown MD 21620 - 410-778-6890

Janes United Methodist Church (1914)
Cross Street, Chestertown, MD 21620

Joshua Chapel United Methodist Church (1839)
River Road & Old Morgnec Road, Chestertown, MD 21620

Olivet United Methodist Church (approx. 1880)
Worton, MD 21678

MONTGOMERY COUNTY

Boyd's Negro School House - 1950 White Ground Road
A restored one-room schoolhouse (1896-1936) complete with furnishing of literature on the school and community.

Josiah Henson - Bethesda, MD
The life of Josiah Henson, a Black plantation slave in northern Bethesda, became a focal point in the abolitionist movement. Henson, who kept a diary of his harsh treatment, was the model for the principal character in Harriet Beeches Stowe's novel, Uncle Tom's Cabin.

HISTORIC CHURCHES: Like many other communities where slavery was practiced, Montgomery County had an influx of churches after the slaves were freed. Serving as the hub of those developing communities, these churches nurtured and took care of members' spiritual and social needs. Many provided non-traditional services including insurance, educational assistance, and funeral expenses which were unavailable to non-White's at that time.

- Montgomery Chapel; Hyattstown, MD; organized 1884.
- Sharpe Street United Methodist; Sandy Spring, MD; organized 1822.
- Poplar Grove Baptist Church; Darnestown, MD.
- Emory Grove United Methodist Church; Gaithersburg, MD, organized 1871.
- Zion A.M.E. Church. This predecessor to the existing Clinton A.M.E. Church was located on the east side of N. Washington St. in Rockville.
- Gililean Fisherman's Temple. Stood on N. Washington St. (currently Hickman's Exxon). Although not a church, this local chapter of a statewide

organization served the many needs of the Black community including funeral expenses, burial grounds, and social cooperation.
- Jerusalem M.E. Church; Wood Lane; founded by Quakers in the early 1900's this congregation later split over the issue of slavery during the Civil War. Part of the membership started what is now the Rockville United Methodist Church on W. Montgomery Ave.

PRINCE GEORGE'S COUNTY

The county was created in April of 1696 out of land formerly belonging to Charles and Calvert counties. In the Metropolitan areas of our nation's capital there is no other area so full of African-American heritage. The county records are extremely accurate on all matters pertaining to the early slave trade from West Africa and Goree Island. While today very little remains of the physical evidence of this early history, oral history and recorded fact by county record have made a fine contribution to the writing of Bianca P. Floyd who created RECORDS AND RECOLLECTIONS, a book for the Maryland National Capital Park and Planning Commission. Available by writing M-NCPPC, Black History Program, 4302 Baltimore Avenue, Bladensburg, MD 20710 (301-779-2011) Price: $15.75

Bowie State College, Bowie, MD
This college is hailed as one of the educational facilities continuously serving Blacks in the state. It was featured in a study by the Afro-American Institute for Historic Preservation and Community Development, and recommended to be placed in the National Register of Historic Places.

Butler House, 6407 Oxon Hill Road, Oxon Hill, MD
This is one of the few houses in the county built by and for a Black family. It was built around 1850 and is an example of the progress made by a free Black family in the mid-19th century.

The Calvert Mansion
Riverdale Plantation, 4811 Riverdale Road, Riverdale, MD
Adam Francis Plummer made shoes, among other chores, while a house slave to George H. Calvert, Lord Baltimore on the "Riverdale," on the plantation. The mansion, but not the slave quarters is listed on the Prince George's Historic Sites and District Register.

Old Clements House, 46th Street, Bladensburg, MD
Built in 1760 by a white man, it is the only frame house left from this time period. In 1890 it was deeded to two Black men.

College Park Airport Museum/The Columbia Air Center at Croom, 6709 Cpl. Frank Scott Dr., College Pk. 20740 , (301) 779-2011
The museum exhibit is a commemoration of the life and career of John W. Greene who was described in FLASH MAGAZINE as being nothing short of being among America's top ranked pilots in the science of air navigation. In 1941, it was the only black owned airport open in Prince

George's County. Greene was issued a commercial pilot's license in 1933, the second black man to qualify. The airport's history as a flying school and training center is available at the museum.

Croom Airport and Slave Cabins, Patuxent River Pk., Croom, MD
This area was once the site of former slave quarters and a grass-strip airport run by Black aviators.

Gibbons Methodist Church
14107 Gibbons Church Road, Brandywine, MD
A Methodist congregation was established by new settlers in 1884. Only the education building and the cemetery remain from the original church which was built in 1889. Deeded to Black settlers by James H.S. Gibbons, a white farmer in Brandywine, the church established the foundation for the Black community in the area.

Jeremiah Hawkins, North Brentwood, MD
Jeremiah Hawkins was from a family of former slaves. In 1920 he became the first Black from Maryland to serve as a delegate to the Republican National Convention. He also became the first mayor of the state's first municipality, North Brentwood.

Lincoln Community, Lanham, MD
This was likely one of the first Black suburbs. A Methodist Church and several turn-of-the-century houses still remain.

Melford House and Outbuildings, Mitchellville, MD
One of the four wooden outbuildings has been identified as former slave quarters. The Melford House is one of the oldest and most architecturally important because of its semi-circular tower.

St. Mary's Beneficial Society Hall and Home of James E. Diggs
14825 Pratt Street, Upper Marlboro, MD
Built in 1888, the Hall has been the center of Black activities for over a century. This is a good example of the fact that churches were frequently the only community structures Blacks could build and usually became the center of their religious and social life.

St. Paul's Methodist Church, 6634 St. Barnabas Road, Oxon Hill, MD
This church is believed to have one of the oldest Black congregations in the United States.

William Sidney Pittman House
505 Eastern Avenue, Fairmount Heights., MD
A Black architect and son-in-law to Booker T. Washington, Pittman's Black architectural firm became the first to win a federal contract. The contract was to build the $70,000 Negro Building at the National Tricentennial Exposition at Jamestown, VA in 1907. He also founded the Fairmount Heights Improvement Co.

African-American Attractions & Historical Sites

Cupid Plummer, Riverdale, MD
 Cupid Plummer earned his and his wife's freedom by fighting in his master's place in the Revolutionary War. His grandson, Adam, was taught to read by a Black Methodist preacher. Adam was a slave for the Calverts.

Poplar Neck Plantation, Frank Tippet Road
 (6 miles Southeast of Upper Marlboro) This land, once a large plantation, was the site of one of Maryland's best-recorded slave conspiracies, and one of the few where names of the ring leaders have come down through history. The land was featured in a study by the Afro-American Institute for Historic Preservation and Community Development.

Overseer's House on Bacon Hall
5611 Old Crain Highway, Upper Marlboro, MD
 Built before 1750, this one and a half story red frame house is the oldest such structure in the county. The house possibly served as a slave overseer's house and perhaps as slaves' quarters for a tobacco farm before the Civil War.

Riverdale Slave Quarters, 4811 Riverdale Road, Riverdale, MD
 The Riverdale Slave Quarters is home to the historic division of the Maryland National Capital Park and Planning Commission.

Seaton A.M.E. Church, 5503 Lincoln Avenue, Lanham, MD
 Named after a Lincoln community resident, Dr. Daniel P. Seaton, this church is the center of the small, predominately Black community.

Spriggs Family Plantation Houses, Slave Quarters and Outbuildings, Northampton, MD
 The ruins of two old slave cabins are a significant and rare archeological find. Few slave sites have offered the unique opportunity for careful excavation and the study of slave life on a documented site, as these structures do. One of the cabins has a fireplace that bears the hand print of a child.

Wormley House, 7533 Ardwick-Ardmore Road, Landover Hills, MD
 James Wormley operated one of the most successful, elegant hotels in Washington, D.C., located at 15th and H Streets, N.W. Opened in 1871, it had an elevator, telephones and a heating system.

St. Mary's County

800 Acre Outdoor Museum, 2 hours south of Washington, D.C. includes a memorial to Mathias de Sousa, the first African settler to arrive in Maryland. 1-301-862-0990 or 800-327-9023

Slave Cabin (1830) - Sotterley Plantation (1710)

At one time Sotterley was a 890 acre tobacco plantation with over 86 slaves. It is located off Route 245 near Route 235 in Hollywood, Maryland. There is a wooden slave cabin still intact. Ms. Agnes Cullum, a Maryland historian, great-grandfather was a slave here. Sotterley served as a colonial port of entry and a 19th century steamboat landing. George Plater, III, the sixth governor of Maryland once owned Sotterley.

SOMERSET COUNTY

Oriole was a bustling town of former slaves turned farmers. Some farmed their own land, but most helped harvest crops. Oyster harvest were at their peak. Canneries were booming and farmers found ready markets for their tomatoes, sweet potatoes, strawberries and other crops. Some Blacks were skilled carpenters, building their own skipjacks and sloping farmhouses.

ST. JAMES METHODIST EPISCOPAL CHURCH

Was one of the oldest African American structures in Somerset County. It was built in 1885 by the sons and daughters of former slaves.

Windsor's Restaurant - Crisfield, MD

As a result of the "sit-in" in which Anthony Ward, Honnes Cane, Louise Whittington and Blancia Cottman participated, the owner of Windsor's Restaurant, Homer Windsor, opened his restaurant to the Black population of the area. This was the first integrated food establishment in the county.

University of Maryland-Eastern Shore, Princess Anne, MD

The University of Maryland Eastern Shore was founded as the Delaware Academy of the Delaware Conference of the Methodist Episcopal Church at Princess Anne. Acquired by the state in 1919, it later became the Maryland State College, a division of the University of Maryland. It acquired its current name in 1970.

TALBOT COUNTY

Birthplace of Frederick Douglass - Tuckahoe Neck Area, MD

There is an historical marker for Douglass near the Tuckahoe Bridge on the Talbot County side of the Tuckahoe River.

African-American Attractions & Historical Sites

Frederick Douglass School - St. Michael's, MD
The original Frederick Douglass School is now a home for the elderly and has been renamed the St. Michael House..

Coulbourne and Jewett Crab and Oyster Packing Company
St. Michael's, MD - Though no longer in existence, this early Black business was founded in St. Michaels and the owners introduced the system for the grading and packing of crab meat.

Freedom Friends Lodge/Cultural Arts Center
102 S. Freemont Street, St. Michael, MD
Chartered and constructed in 1867, oldest Lodge still existing in Maryland served as a meeting hall for Blacks

WASHINGTON COUNTY

Antietam National Battlefield(NPS) - (301) 432-5124
The bloodiest conflict of the Civil War left over 23, 000 men killed or wounded. It was the turning point needed for Abraham Lincoln to announce his Emancipation Proclamation. It was to come on September 22, 1862 just five days after the battle left Lee in retreat. No Black Union troops took part in the conflict, but the effect on the lives of African-Americans is unmistakable. Located just one mile north of Sharpsburg, the park is operated by the National Park Service. Open daily 8:30am-5:00pm

Slave Auction Blocks, Church and East Main Streets, Sharpsburg, MD
This is one of four sites where slave auction blocks were located in the county. The original one for this location still exists, the other three have been moved. The main auction spot was in front of the county court house where unclaimed runaway salves were sold.

Fort Frederick, Fort Frederick, MD
Nathan Williams, a free black, owned and farmed this land. Williams was considered the second wealthiest Black in the county. The land had been owned by Blacks for 50 years, who sold it in 1910 to the federal government. Fort Frederick State Park is located between Indian Springs and Big Springs on Route 56 in Washington County.

Williamsport School, Williamsport, MD
This was the location of the first colored public school in the county. Mrs. Elizabeth Nelson Thomas taught there in 1869.

Doleman Black Heritage Museum
540 N. Locust Street, Hagerstown, MD 21740, 301-739-8185
Mrs. Doleman has been researching Black History of Washington County since 1972. Five rooms of her and her husband Charles home have been turned over to display Black History memorabilia. Special arrangements may be made to view the "museum".

African-American Attractions & Historical Sites

WICOMICO COUNTY

John Wesley M.E. Church
Broad and Ellen Streets, Salisbury, MD
> This Church is the oldest on the Eastern Shore and one of the oldest in Maryland. In 1837, Livin Houston, George Ullett, Major Toadnine, George James, and Elijah Pinkett, all freed slaves, organized and began to hold religious meetings in a red slab building on the property of William Williams. The property was purchased in 1838 and the Church was first incorporated in 1876.

Charles H. Chipman Cultural Center
E. Church & Broad Streets, Salisbury, MD - 410-860-9290
> Formerly the John Wesley AME Church. This historical site was originally purchased in the year 1838 by a group of five local freedmen. It represents the oldest known African-American congregation on the Eastern Shore. It is possibly the oldest in Maryland. Current plans call for the development of a cultural and civic center to serve the needs of the community and provide a setting for recitals, lectures and permanent exhibits of the Eastern Shore's Black History and the 19th century black identity. The City of Salisbury is carrying out plans to surround the renovated church with a beautiful 3 acre park as a focal point for community activity.

WORCESTER COUNTY

Birthplace of Charles Tindley - Sinepauxent Area, Berlin, MD
> Charles Schert Tindley was born in 1856 in Berlin, MD. He was a slave and orphaned at an early age. He learned to read at seventeen. He received his license to preach in 1885. It was due to his outstanding ability as a preacher that his congregations grew rapidly and his followers were many. At his funeral, 3,200 persons attended the service and more than 8,000 passed by his burial.

Tindley's Memorial Park - Tindleytown, MD
> This town was named for John Tindley, Charles Tindley's brother. This is where the Old Tindley's Chapel Church was located. The grounds where the Chapel Church once stood are being developed as a Memorial Park. A brick monument from the front steps of the "old" Church has been constructed on the exact spot where the Church once stood.

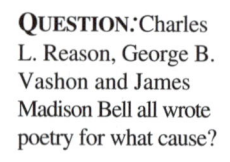

QUESTION: Charles L. Reason, George B. Vashon and James Madison Bell all wrote poetry for what cause?

BLACK FACT

Answer: The abolition of slavery.

Freedom Fighters

MARTIN LUTHER KING, JR. and **MALCOLM X** exchange friendly banter during a chance meeting in the U.S. Senate in Wash., D.C., March 26, 1964. King, president of the Southern Christian Leadership Conference, and Malcolm X, president of the Muslim Mosque, Inc. and former national representative of the Nation of Islam, had observed the 1964 civil-rights bill debate from separate sections of the visitors' gallery. Afterward King addressed reporters in a nearby conference room, then left by one door, while Malcolm X, who had listened from the back row, slipped through another and met him in the corridor. "Well, Malcolm, good to see you," King said, smiling and extending his hand. "Good to see you," the grinning Muslim nationalist replied. As they shook hands, photographers called out "Hold it" to capture the event. Malcolm bent toward King and said, "Now you're going to be investigated." It was their first and, apparently, only meeting. Malcolm X was assassinated in New York City, Feb. 21, 1965; King in Memphis, April 4, 1968.

> The goal has always been the same, with the approaches to it as different as mine and Dr. Martin Luther King's non-violent marching, that dramatizes the brutality and the evil of the white man against defenseless Blacks. And in the climate of this country today, it is anybody's guess which of the "extremes" in approach to the Black man's problems might **personally** meet a fatal catastrophe first — "nonviolent" Dr. King, or so-called "violent" me. *The Autobiography of Malcolm X*

BALTIMORE CITY

HENRY BAINES: President/CEO of the Nation's largest chain of Black-owned supermarkets, the Stop, Shop & Save Supermarkets.

DR. SAMUEL BANKS: The 20th century version of Dr. Carter G. Woodson was best personified by the life of Baltimore educator Dr. Samuel L. Banks who passed on July 19, 1995. Dr. Banks was truly a scholar and a gentleman. He was also a mentor, motivator, an activist, a positive influence, a leader, a prolific writer, a lecturer, a family man and a historian with few equals. Dr. Banks served as the Director of the Department of Compensatory and Funded Programs in Baltimore City Public Schools and as an Adjunct Professor of Education at Morgan State University.

JARED R. BEADS: (1928-1996) A/K/A *"The Human Running Machine"*: Beads was born in Mt. Winans in Southwest Baltimore. Beads was a marathon runner who earned a place in the Guinness Book of World Records in 1969 after running non-stop for 121 miles, 440 yards in 22 hours and 27 minutes.

NICHOLAS BIDDLE: The first blood shed by Union soldiers in the Civil War was shed in Baltimore in 1861 by Nicholas Biddle.

EUBIE BLAKE: Born in East Baltimore, Eubie became a famous ragtime pianist, vaudevillian and composer of such Broadway classics as "I'm Just Wild About Harry" and "Memories of You." In 1921 he co-composed Broadway's first black musical, "Schuffle Along." Blake died in 1983 at the illustrious age of 100. In Baltimore, the Eubie Blake National Museum and Cultural Center is a major draw for tourists.

CAB CALLOWAY: Baltimore's most famous entertainer. Known for his recording, "Minnie the Moocher", star of the Royal Theatre. Cab starred in several New York musicals and many motion pictures. An exhibit in his honor is housed at the Coppin State College Library. He was a graduate of the Class of 1928 at Douglass High School.

DR. BENJAMIN CARSON: International Neurosurgeon. Dr. Carson gained international acclaim for leading the team of some 100 medical and surgical professionals in the highly complicated procedure to separate the "Bender" Siamese Twins in 1987. This operation has been recognized as a modern day medical miracle.

Freedom Fighters

Born in 1951 in Detroit, Michigan, Dr. Carson went on to obtain degrees from Yale University in 1973 and a medical doctorate degree from the University of Michigan School of Medicine in 1977. Dr. Carson currently serves as the Director of the Division of Pediatric Neurosurgery at the Johns Hopkins University and Hospital. Considered as a top leader in his field, Dr. Carson has authored more than sixty-five medical publications and conducts numerous lectures, and has appeared on countless network television and radio shows. His life story is presented in his best selling autobiography Gifted Hands.

ALBERT J. CASSELL: Architect, 1885-1969, formerly head of the architecture department at Howard University, Cassell was born in Baltimore, and studied architecture at the School of Architecture, Cornell University. As an architect, he worked on the construction of five buildings at Tuskegee Institute. As a draftsman he was responsible for designing an industrial plan for the manufacture of silk. He later served as the architect for Howard University's gymnasium and athletic field (1924), the College of Medicine (1926), three women's dormitory buildings (1931) and his most outstanding project at Howard, the Founders Library (1946). His largest project was the Mayfair Mansion, a $5 million apartment complex in Washington, D.C. His work appears elsewhere in this country and in Africa.

HARRY CUMMINGS: The first Black to serve in elective office in Maryland was Harry Scythe Cummings who won the Republican seat in the Baltimore City Council in 1891. He was also the first Black to graduate from the University of Maryland Law School in 1889. Mr. Cummings gave the seconding speech for the nomination of Theodore Roosevelt at the Republican Convention in 1904.

LEON DAY (1916-1995): Born on October 30, 1916. Negro Leagues baseball player, 22 year career, great pitcher, beat the legendary Satchel Paige 3 out of 4 times, won five championships, after being out of baseball for 39 years Day was elected to the National Baseball Hall of Fame on March 7, 1995. Tragically, he passed on March 13, 1995.

ELLA FITZGERALD: Although born in Newport News, Virginia, Ella has been a Baltimore fixture forever. A marvelous vocalist, Ms. Fitzgerald sang with the top musicians including Count Basie, Eubie Blake, and Chick Webb. She recorded hundreds of hit records with the tune titled "A Tisket A Tasket" being the most popular.

Freedom Fighters

E. FRANKLIN FRAZIER (1894-1962): The father and leading pioneer in Black sociology. Frazier authored several books including his most influential "The Black Bourgeoisie" (1957). Frazier was born in Baltimore, MD on September 24, 1894. He graduated from Howard with honors in 1916, received an M. A. from Clark University in 1920 and obtained his Ph.D. in Sociology in 1931 from the University of Chicago. He taught at Morehouse, Fisk, Atlanta University and from 1934 to 1959 served as head of Howard University's Department of Sociology. He became president of the predominantly white American Sociological Society in 1948. Frazier died in Washington, D.C. on May 17, 1962.

HARLOW FULLWOOD, JR.: Baltimore's Best Charitable Giver. After retiring as a Baltimore City Police Officer, Mr. Fullwood and his wife, Elnora opened several successful Kentucky Fried Chicken franchises. Fullwood became known for providing employment opportunities for young people and for giving young people a second chance. Yearly, the Fullwood Breakfast is attended by thousands of his supporters. The Fullwoods have donated over $500,000 to non-profit organizations and needy students.

JOE GANS: First Black to own an automobile in Baltimore, Baltimore's first boxing champ, lightweight.

GEORGE ALEXANDER HACKETT (1806-1870): An early activist who lived through 12 assassination threats and was an important political leader of his day, helping to establish the Douglass Institute.

DR. CARLA HAYDEN - TOP LIBRARIAN IN THE U.S.
Baltimore can now boast that it has the nation's top librarian. She is Dr. Carla Hayden, Director of the Enoch Pratt Library who received the National Librarian of the Year Award for 1995.

Dr. Hayden is the first African American and the first Pratt librarian to receive the Library Journal Award. She has received three degrees including a Bachelors in 1973 from Roosevelt University in Chicago, a Masters in 1977 from the University of Chicago's Graduate Library School and in 1987 a Ph.D also from the University of Chicago.

She is a member of the American Library Association and the International Women's Forum.

Freedom Fighters

RAYMOND HAYSBERT, SR.: The Dean of Baltimore's Businessmen. Retired President of Parks Sausage. Mr. Haysbert has been named Entrepreneur of the Year. A teacher and mentor, Mr. Haysbert is a member of the President's Roundtable. He is also the CEO of the Forum Caterers, a multi-million dollar business.

BILLIE HOLIDAY: Born Eleanora Fagan on April 7, 1915 in Baltimore. Billie Holiday has been called the greatest jazz singer ever. Lady Day went to New York City and on to jazz fame becoming known for ballads such as "God Bless the Child" and "Strange Fruit". She first recorded with Benny Goodman in 1933 and later with Count Basie and Teddy Wilson. Along with charming crowds at nightclubs such as the Cafe Society and the Cotton Club, Holiday performed at Baltimore's famous Royal Theater.

CATHERINE HUGHES: CEO and Owner of the Radio One which consists of several radio stations in Baltimore, Washington, D.C. and Atlanta, Georgia. She employs over 200 people.

Her son, Alfred Liggins, Jr. a graduate of the prestigious Wharton School of Business serves as the President and General Manager of Radio One.

Originally from Omaha, Nebraska, Ms. Hughes relocated to the District of Columbia in 1971 to become a lecturer at the School of Communications at Howard University. As General Manager of Howard's radio station WHUR, she increased the station's revenue from $250,000 to over $3 million.

Ms. Hughes created the phenomenal format known as the "Quiet Storm". Acquiring WOL & WOLB AM in 1980, Hughes pioneered another innovative format for radio "Black Talk". With the theme "Information Is Power" WOL AM has become the most listened to talk show in the Baltimore/Washington area.

LILLIE CARROLL JACKSON: President of Baltimore's NAACP chapter from 1935 to 1969. Jackson extended the city's bureau to the largest chapter in the country by 1946. She fought to desegregate the city's public and private facilities, and worked for equal opportunities and the election of African-Americans to public office.

JOSHUA JOHNSON: America's first Black portrait painter of renown, Johnson lived and actively worked in Baltimore from 1765 to 1830. He received national acclaim with portraits of prominent Marylanders;

his portraits captured their likeness in the colonial two dimensional style. For a time, Johnson's studio was located near the present day Morris Mechanic Theater at Charles & Baltimore Streets where there is a marker. His paintings can be viewed in several art museums including the Metropolitan in New York, the Gallery in Washington, D.C. and the Maryland Historical Society on downtown Baltimore.

GREAT BLACKS IN WAX FOUNDERS
Drs. Elmer Martin and JoAnne Martin

MOTHER LANGE (1784-1882): She founded the first U.S. Catholic school for Black children in Baltimore in 1828, and a year later, the first religious order for women of African descent - the Oblate Sisters of Providence. The order still operates a high school, St. Frances Academy on East Chase Street and a Day Care Center at its motherhouse, 701 Gun Road in Catonsville. She was born in 1784 in Haiti and migrated to Fells Point in 1817. She taught free and slave Black children to read in her home. To become a nun she had to start her own order. Mother Lange is one of three individuals who could become the first African-American Saint designated by the Vatican.

REGINALD LEWIS: A native of East Baltimore, Reginald Lewis became the President and CEO of TLC Beatrice Foods, Inc., the nation's largest Black owned business.

CATHERINE M.F. LYLES (1906-1996): Ms. Lyles founded the first African-American Girl Scout Troop #502 at Sharon Baptist Church in Baltimore. She was a member there for 76 years. She also taught in Baltimore City Public Schools for 34 years. Ms. Lyles was the daughter of Pullman Porter. She graduated from Frederick Douglass High School in 1923 and from Coppin Normal School.

THURGOOD MARSHALL (1908-1993): Thurgood Marshall was an Attorney, Judge, U.S. Solicitor General. Supreme Court Justice.

Thurgood Marshall was born in Baltimore on July 2, 1908 and passed on January 24, 1993. He was born just six months before the founding of the NAACP. He was the great-grandson of slaves. A graduate of Lincoln University, a Black college in Oxford, Pennsylvania, he was denied admission to the University of Maryland Law School. In 1933 Marshall received his law degree from Howard University in Washington, D.C. In 1938, Marshall succeeded his mentor, Charles H. Houston as the head of the NAACP's Legal Defense Fund, Inc.,

Prior to becoming the first African-American Supreme Court Justice in 1967, he gained national prominence for his appearance before the Supreme Court, arguing against school desegregation as Chief Counsel to the NAACP. On May 17, 1954 Justice Marshall won his most significant case in "Brown v. Board of Education".

Altogether, Thurgood Marshall won twenty-nine of thirty-two cases before the U.S. Supreme Court. Some of his most pivotal cases were "Sweat v. Painter, McLaurin v. Oklahoma State Regents, Brown v. Board of Education, and University of Maryland v. Murray.

Marshall once said "Equal means getting the same thing at the same time and in the same place". The Marshall legacy is one of promoting racial equality and fighting intolerance through legal battles fought constitutionally and through the court system.

ESTHER MCCREADY - *A Genuine First*

This Baltimore City native was the first Black to earn a nursing diploma from the University of Maryland at Baltimore.

KWESI MFUME: (pronounced Kwah-EE-see Oom-FOO-may) Kweisi served ten years as a Representative of Maryland's 7th Congressional District, to which he was first elected in 1986. He was born, raised and educated in the Baltimore area, and it was there that he followed his dreams to impact society and shape a more humane public policy.

Congressman Mfume, whose African name means "conquering son of kings," became politically active as a freshman in college. He graduated magna cum laude from Morgan State University in 1976 and later returned as Adjunct Professor, teaching courses in political science and communications. He earned a masters degree from Johns Hopkins University with a concentration in International Studies.

As Mfume's community involvement grew, so did his popularity. He translated that approval into a grass-roots election victory when he won a seat on the Baltimore City Council in 1979. Mfume is President and CEO of the National Association for the Advancement of Colored People.

CLARENCE MITCHELL, JR.: A lawyer and civil rights leader, Clarence Mitchell served as executive director of the Washington, DC branch of the NAACP. Clarence M. Mitchell, Jr. served in the Washington Bureau of the NAACP for 32 years, starting as labor secretary and becoming Director of the Bureau in 1950. In July 1969, Mr. Mitchell was awarded the Springarn Medal at the National Convention of the NAACP for his outstanding efforts in obtaining passage of Civil Rights bills such as: the 1957 Civil Rights Act which gave the Attorney General of the United States the power to institute civil suits to protect the right to vote; the Fair Housing Act of 1968 which outlaws discrimination in the sale and rental of housing; and the United States Civil Rights Commission; the 1964 law forbidding discrimination in places of public accommodation, establishing an Equal Opportunity Agency.

Clarence M. Mitchell graduated from Lincoln University, Pennsylvania. He completed his graduate work at Atlanta University and the University of Minnesota and his Juris Doctorate at the University of Maryland Law School.

PARREN J. MITCHELL: Some call him "Baltimore's living legend", others still refer to him as Congressman, others just say P.J. Parren Mitchell is also known as "Mr. Minority Business" or the "Godfather of Minority Business." Simply, he is the Man, without fear, a true American hero, a statesman like no other.

In 1970, he was elected Maryland's first Black Congressman. Mr. Mitchell, in 1976 created and passed legislation to establish minority business set asides on government contracts. Mitchell helped organize the Congressional Black Caucus. He sponsored, as well as pushed countless bills designed to benefit minority businesses.

Although retired, Parren stills provides leadership in his role as Chairman of the Minority Business Enterprise Legal Defense and Education Fund, Inc., an organization that will go down in history as "The Justice Department For Minority Business".

JUANITA JACKSON MITCHELL: CIVIL RIGHTS ACTIVIST, daughter of Dr. Lillie Carroll Jackson. First Black Female Lawyer in the State of Maryland.

CAMAY MURPHY: Camay Murphy is the oldest of five daughters of the late stage personality, Cab Calloway. Having chosen a career in education with a B.S. from New York University and an M.A. from the University of the District of Columbia, she retired as Principal of an award winning school in Arlington, Virginia - Ashlawn School. Ashlawn was the first elementary school in Virginia to institute a jazz theory and performance program.

ISSAC MYERS (1835-1891): Myers was a Baltimore native, born of free Black parents in the year 1835. At the age of 16 he became an apprentice ship's caulker. In the days of wooden-hulled ships this was a very important job, one that Myers shared with Frederick Douglass, who had been so employed earlier. Myers went on to become a supervisor in one of the largest shipyards in bustling Baltimore Harbor. After the Civil War, Blacks were being eliminated from the ranks of shipyard workers. Myers, to counter the effort, raised $10,000 from among Blacks in Maryland and set up the Chesapeake Bay Shipyard & Drydock Company, a Black owned and controlled shipyard. It was a success and led to the establishment of an all Black union "The Baltimore Caulker Trade Society". The shipyard even won U.S. contracts and within five years Myers paid off all the company's debts. Isaac Myers created the National Labor Union for Blacks in 1869. He was prominent in Republican politics until his death in 1891. It can only be surmised that his shipyard was located on the present site of Baltimore's glittering Inner Harbor.

Isaac Myers was a pillar of Bethel A.M.E. Church. Myers became one of the first postal inspectors assigned to criminal detection in U.S.P.O. history.

NORMAN E. ROSS: He had been the subject of an experimental program to test the feasibility of a mixed situation at Wilmington Music School in Wilmington, Delaware.

Realizing the lack of cultural and artistic advantages for African-Americans in Baltimore, he enthusiastically organized what was to be one of the most successful programs of the Model Cities era. In his tenure as director of the Cultural Arts Program, Mr. Ross sought to bring a wide spectrum of cultural advantages to African-Americans. He organized summer enrichment programs for young people. In 1996 after 20 years of service, Mr. Ross retired as Executive Director of the Eubie Blake Cultural Center.

ALICE G. PINDERHUGHES: Mrs. Pinderhughes, who received her undergraduate degree from Coppin in 1942, headed the Baltimore City Public Schools through much of the turbulent 1980's as the city's first woman superintendent.

KURT L. SCHMOKE: Kurt L. Schmoke was born in Baltimore on September 1, 1949. He attended City High School and earned a degree in history from Yale University in 1971. After attending Oxford University as a Rhodes Scholar, he received his law degree in 1976 from the Harvard Law School.

In 1977, he joined President Carter's White House Domestic Policy staff. In 1978, Mr. Schmoke returned to Baltimore as an Assistant United States Attorney, where he prosecuted narcotic and white collar crime.

In November 1982 Mr. Schmoke was elected State's Attorney for Baltimore City, which is the chief prosecuting office of the City.

Kurt Schmoke became the first elected Black Mayor of Baltimore on November 3, 1987. In his inaugural address on December 8, 1987, Mayor Schmoke announced his intention to make Baltimore "The City that Reads."

Mayor Schmoke was elected on November 1991 to his second term. A month later, in his swearing-in speech, the mayor pledged to make education, public safety, and the environment his administration's top priorities. In 1995 Mayor Schmoke was elected to a third term of the City of Baltimore.

Mayor Schmoke and his wife Patricia, reside in Baltimore with their two children, Gregory and Katherine.

MARY CARTER SMITH: - Maryland's Famed Griot (1919). Mary Carter Smith was an elementary school teacher and a librarian in the inner-city schools of Baltimore for 31 years. During this time, "she told and read stories, sang songs, and wrote and recited poetry" -- all centered on her African heritage. She has dedicated herself to storytelling on a full time basis and has entranced thousands of people. She carries on -- with "her messages of love and understanding" -- the best of what the great oral traditions of Africa have to offer the world. In 1983, she became Maryland's official Griot.

ELISHA TYSON (1749-1824): A Quaker Philanthropist who was instrumental in stopping the kidnapping of Blacks in Baltimore and he was helpful in establishing Black churches.

Freedom Fighters

KATHY WATERS: As Manager of Maryland's MARC Commuter Rail System, Waters is responsible for directing and managing all activities of the rapidly expanding commuter rail service, which currently serves five million passengers each year.
Waters, 46, the first African-American woman in Maryland's history to manage a commuter rail service. In fact, she is the highest ranking Black woman employed by the MTA (an agency of the Maryland Department of Transportation), and one of the few minority women in the U.S. to manage a commuter rail service.

WILLIAM WATKINS (1800-1858): Watkins was the first Baltimore Black who wrote for abolition newspaper in the north and was the uncle of Black poet Frances Ellen Watkins.

FRANCIS ELLEN WATKINS: The first published Black woman novelist in America was born in Baltimore in 1925. She was the first Black woman to have her works published in The Atlantic Monthly. Harper attended a school for Blacks at the site of the present day Baltimore Convention Center.

CHICK WEBB: Born in Baltimore 1909 was known as "Harlem's King of Drums". He cut his first recording (Jungle Man and Dog Bottom) in 1929 with his jungle band, but his theme song was "I May Be Wrong." He also introduced the world to Ella Fitzgerald. Webb died in 1939 at the age of 30 at Johns Hopkins Hospital.

VERDA M.F. WELCOME: Senator Verda Welcome, 1907-1990, was a teacher, a pioneer in the civil rights movement, a trail blazing legislator for a quarter of a century and a creative political organizer.

STATE SENATOR LARRY YOUNG: State Senator Larry Young, Democrat, 44th District, has been called the hardest working legislator in the State of Maryland - unbought, unbossed, always responsive, a workaholic--a true people person. He served in the House of Delegates for 13-1/2 years, 1975-1988. He chaired the House Environmental Matters Committee from 1982-1986; chaired the (AELR) Committee from 1987-1988; and City House Delegation in 1987. He was appointed to the State Senate in February 1988 and then reelected in 1990 and 1994. He will serve as chairman of the Maryland Black Legislative Caucus from 1997-98.

Freedom Fighters

BATTLE OF BALTIMORE

Spanish-American War of 1812

WILLIAM WILLIAMS

Williams was a native Marylander slave. He had run away from his owner Benjamin Oden, in the Spring of 1814. On April 14, 1814, Williams was enlisted as a private in the U.S. Army and was assigned to the 38th U.S. Infantry Regiment. Federal law at the time prohibited the enlistment of slaves into the army because they "could make no valid contract with the government." The officer who enlisted Williams did not question him.

In early September, 1814, the 38th U.S. Infantry was ordered to march to Fort McHenry. During the bombardment, Williams was severely wounded, having his leg "blown off by a cannonball." He was taken to the Baltimore Hospital, where he died two months later.

Williams was not the only black man to serve in the armed services at this time. There are numerous records of Black sailors. George Roberts, a free black, served on the privateers <u>Chasseur</u> ("Pride of Baltimore") and <u>Sarah Ann</u>. Charles Ball was a Seaman in Commodore Joshua Barney's U.S. Chesapeake Flotilla who later published his memoirs in 1836.

Gabriel Roulson was an Ordinary Seaman on the U.S. Sloop of War <u>Ontario</u>. Baltimore also had many skilled free blacks who, as naval mechanics, sailmakers, riggers, carpenters and ship caulkers, helped build naval ships and privateers that would bring war to the British merchant fleet and navy. Many of these men and slaves helped construct gun carriages and build defenses.

Williams was unique because he served in the U.S. Army, a branch of the armed services that was almost exclusively white at the time.

24th Infantry - U.S. Army

FREEDOM FIGHTERS Beyond BALTIMORE

ANNE ARUNDEL COUNTY

WILLIAM H. BUTLER: The first Black to be elected to the Annapolis City Council in 1893.

CHARLES DOUGLASS: Charles Douglass founded the Highland Beach Community, located just south of Annapolis. The son of the famous freedom fighter, Frederick Douglass, Charles brought 40 acres of beach front land in response to the segregation he and his wife Laura experienced at the Bay Ridge resort outside of Annapolis. Douglass developed a private Black community that would be a summer retreat for friends and family.

KUNTE KINTE/ALEX HALEY: A Kunte Kinte marker is located at the Annapolis City dock. Each year a three day festival is held in honor of Kunte Kinte in Annapolis. Alex Haley (1921-1992) traced his ancestry back to an African prince named Kunte Kinte. Haley discovered that the slave ship that brought Kunte Kinte from West Africa to America had landed in Annapolis in 1767. Haley wrote several books including the famous "Roots", "The Saga of an American Family" and "The Autobiography of Malcolm X". In 1977 Haley's book, Roots was made into a TV mini-series that attracted over 130 million viewers.

MAJOR F. RIDDICK, JR.: was appointed Chief of Staff for the State of Maryland in January of 1995. As Chief of Staff he is responsible for overseeing and managing the daily operations of State Government.

Riddick was raised in Chesapeake, Virginia, he received a Bachelor of Arts Degree from Virginia Polytechnic Institute and State University in 1972 and his Masters of Urban and Public Administration in 1973.

QUESTION: The wooden clock he constructed was probably the first to be built in the United States

BLACK FACT

Answer: Benjamin Banneker

Freedom Fighters

BALTIMORE COUNTY

BENJAMN BANNEKER (1731-1806): A parade is held in his honor in Baltimore County each year. Benjamin Banneker was born free in the Ellicott's Mills section of Baltimore county, Maryland on November 9, 1731. Banneker was the only child of a free mulatto mother and an African father, who had purchased his freedom from slavery.

A contemporary of George Washington, Banneker used his renown as a mathematician, astronomer, surveyor, and writer to champion the cause of enslaved Blacks.

In 1753, Banneker produced the first clock ever built in the United States. It was made entirely of wood and each gear was made by hand. The clock kept perfect time, striking every hour, for more than forty years.

His aptitude in mathematics and knowledge of astronomy enabled him to predict the solar eclipse that took place on April 14, 1789. In 1792, Benjamin Banneker was the first African to publish an almanac, which was widely read and became a major reference for farmers.

Banneker, the first African American appointee by President George Washington was a surveyor. He helped in selecting the sites for the U.S. Capitol building, the White House and other federal buildings. When the chairman of the civil engineering team, Major L'Enfant, abruptly resigned and returned to France with the plans, Banneker's photographic memory enabled him to reproduce them in their entirety.

The nation's capital, Washington, D.C. was completed and stands today as a monument to Benjamin Banneker's genius.

In September 1996, a ground breaking ceremony was held at the future site of the Benjamin Banneker Historical Park and Museum.

AUGUSTUS WALLEY - Buffalo Soldier: A slave, a soldier, and a savior of his fellow comrades, Augustus Walley was born in 1856 on Bond Ave. in Baltimore County, Maryland. Although born a slave in America, Mr. Walley would rise above what others thought "his proper place" and in 1881 Walley received the highest, most coveted award that the United States of America could bestow to a military man - THE CONGRESSIONAL AWARD OF HONOR! He spent thirty years in the 9th and 10th Calvary. He fought the Indians in August 1881 at Cuchillo Negro Mountains, New Mexico. Walley

Freedom Fighters

participated in Teddy Roosevelt's famous charge up San Juan Hill, Cuba. He retired as a First Sargeant in 1907. It wasn't until 1995, thanks to the efforts of Mr. Houston Wedlock, that Walley's family discovered that he was a national hero, a Congressional Medal of Honor recipient.

Calvert County

C. Vernon Gray: A native of Calvert County is the only African-American serving on the Howard County Council.

James Harrod: James Harrod was a former slave owned by the Helen family. In 1873 he purchased six acres of land for $210.00 and along with his wife Cecilia, and another former slave, James Wilson established Ben's Creek Community. Lewis Bourne, Peter Gross and Louis and Lidia Brooks were former slaves who settled in Ben's Creek Community.

Joseph Smith, John Rice, George and Sarah Rice, John Gray & his son Thomas, Hezekiah Locks, and Norman Gray all built property in Calvert County.

William Sampson Brooks - Brooks Administrative Center: This building, which currently houses the board of education, was named after William Sampson Brooks. From 1939 until 1975, the building served as a school. Until the mid '60's only Black students attended this school. Brooks, born in Lower Marlboro in 1865, served as a minister in Minneapolis, Chicago, Des Moines, Nashville, St. Louis, Wichita, and Baltimore.

Carroll County

Richard Dixon: Elected in January 1996, Richard N. Dixon is the twenty-second Maryland State Treasurer since the Constitution of 1851, and he is the first African-American to serve in this position. He is also the first treasurer from Western Maryland and is the first Carroll County citizen to serve as a Constitutional officer in over one hundred years. As one of his Constitutional responsibilities, Treasurer Dixon serves as a member of the Board of Public Works, Maryland's highest administrative council, and he is the first African-American to serve on this board as well.

Freedom Fighters

CHARLES COUNTY

MATTHEW HENSON: Matthew Henson was born in Charles County on April 8, 1866. From Baltimore Henson found a job as a cabin boy on a sailing ship where the vessel's captain taught him mathematics and navigation. In 1909 he became the first Black American to reach the North Pole, co-discovering it with Captain Admiral Perry. A tablet in Henson's honor resides in Annapolis and April 6th is "Matthew Henson Day" in Maryland.

JOSIAH HENSON: Born a slave in 1789, south of Baltimore in Charles County, Henson escaped to Canada in 1830. It is there that he became a well-known Methodist preacher and author. It is said that Henson told his life story to Harriet Beecher Stowe, author of "Uncle Tom's Cabin" (published in 1853) and served as the model for the title character. Henson passed in 1883.

DORCHESTER COUNTY

DR. THELMA BANKS COX: Distinguished Educator, Civic Leader, World Traveler, Writer and Humanitarian. Ms. Cox a native Marylander was born on July 21, 1928 and reared in Cambridge, MD on the Eastern Shore. She received her Bachelor of Science degree from Morgan State College at the age of 19. She later earned her Master of Science degree in Education Administration and Supervision from Morgan in 1972. Ms. Cox earned her Ph.D. degree from the Washington, D.C. Center for Minority Studies of the Union Graduate School, Cincinnati, OH with a dissertation on Blacks in Higher Education Governance. Ms. Cox rose from a classroom teacher to become the first Black female Regional Superintendent in the Baltimore City Public Schools. She served 15 years as the Governor's appointee, again the first Black female, to the State Board for Higher Education.

Freedom Fighters

HOME OF HARRIET TUBMAN (1820-1913): Born Araminta Ross on the slave quarters on the Broadas Plantation in Dorchester county, Maryland. Harriet escaped from slavery and made 19 trips back to the south to rescue more than 300 slaves. Called by some the "Black Moses" she was the most famous conductor on the Underground Railroad. During the civil war Harriet Tubman distinguished herself as a nurse, spy and scout in the Union Army. She organized slave intelligence networks behind enemy lines and led scouting raids. She also became the first and possibly the last woman to lead U.S. Army troops in battle. Harriet Tubman died penniless in Auburn, New York on March 10, 1913, nearly 50 years after the Emancipation Proclamation.

FREDERICK COUNTY

CHUCK FOREMAN: Home of former National Football League running back Charles "Chuck" Foreman. Chuck played in several Super Bowls with the Minnesota Vikings.

GARRETT COUNTY

NEMESIS: A National Hero and a Fighter for Freedom, Nemesis was a slave in Garrett County. Negro Mountain in Garrett County is named in his honor. Upon hearing that an Indian War Party was coming across the mountain to attack his slave owner's farm, Nemesis told his "owner" that he would go and fight the Indians but he would not return. Nemesis planned to go on to freedom. Ironically, he died in the battle and Negro Mountain is named in honor of this slave's will to fight and die for freedom.

HOWARD COUNTY

LEOLA DORSEY: A Native of Howard County, Ms. Dorsey was born during the dark days of discrimination and segregation. A strong civil rights advocate, she led the fight to desegregate the Howard County Parent/Teachers Association. She joined the Howard NAACP in 1944. Ms. Dorsey was responsible for the integration of the restaurants along Rout 40. She was the first African-American to run for election to the Howard County Council and the County's Register of Wills. Ms. Leola Dorsey - A True Trailblazer!

C. Vernon Gray: The first African-American to serve on the Howard County Council.

Doris and Claude Ligon: Founders of the Maryland Museum of African Art.

Doris Hillian Ligon, born in Baltimore, Maryland has been a student of traditional African art for approximately 25 years. She possesses a B.A. in Sociology and an M.A. in Art History/Museology from Morgan State University. She has completed Ph.D. level courses in African History at Howard University. For eight years she was a docent at the National Museum of African Art in Washington, D.C.

In 1980 she founded Gallery Ligon, a museum of traditional African art which was eventually to be redesignated the African Art Museum of Maryland.

The African Art Museum of Maryland is one of only three in the United States which is devoted exclusively to traditional African art. It is Columbia, Maryland's first museum and the first of its kind started by an African-American.

Celonia Walden: Howard County's most beloved citizen and community organizer.

Harford County

Ira Aldridge: Born in 1805, Ira grew up in Bel Air, Maryland. Having attended schools in New York and Scotland, by 1833 Aldridge drew large crowds to see him perform Shakespeare. He was the first black person to be knighted. Aldridge died in London in 1867 and has a memorial chair at the Shakespeare Theater in Stratford-upon-Avon.

Kent County

Henry H. Garnet (1815-1882): Garnet was born a slave in Kent County, MD on December 23, 1815. He escaped from slavery with his parents in 1824. He graduated from Onedia Institute, an abolitionist school near Utica, NY in 1840. He studied theology and pastored churches in New York City and Washington, DC.

While attending the National Convention of Colored Citizens in Buffalo, NY in August 1843, Garnet issued his celebrated "Address to the Slaves of the U.S." urging slave revolts and calling for the total annihilation of slavery as a "sin against God". With this address Garnet galvanized a whole nation, black and white abolitionist, slaveholders and slaves, pro and anti-colonizationists-to deal with

America's great sin and lie, slavery. Henry Highland Garnet was named Minister of Liberia in June 1881. He died in Monravia, Liberia on February 13, 1882.

MONTGOMERY COUNTY

NINA CLARK: This former principal of Aspen Hill Elementary School spent her 36 year career in the Montgomery County Public School system as a teacher, teacher specialist and administrator. Since retirement, Mrs. Clarke has researched and written several works dealing with local Black history. In May of 1978, she co-authored "History of the Black Public Schools of Montgomery County, Maryland, 1872-1961."

CELESTINE PRATHER & JESSE HEBRON: After serving honorably in the U.S. Military, Jesse reunited with Celestine and together they built Hebron Press that has served the Black community for the last sixty years. Self taught, Mr. Hebron still uses the traditional typesetting technique that he perfected many years ago. This multi-talented citizen is also an architect (designing the home they have lived in for 60 years) builder and musician.

JOSIAH HENSON: The life of Josiah Henson, a Black plantation slave in northern Bethesda, became a focal point in the abolitionist movement. Henson, who kept a diary of his harsh treatment, was the model for the principal character in Harriet Beecher Stowe's, "Uncle Tom's Cabin."

ROBERT H. HILL: During a time when banks neglected to lend to non-Whites, Bob Hill, the self-taught founder and owner of Sandy Spring Construction Company built and financed (often with no-down payment) over 250 of the more than 500 homes built in and around Montgomery County. Serving as the first African-American on the board of Citizens Building & Loan Association, Mr. Hill influenced many loan and hiring decisions involving Blacks. His many honors include the recent naming of an area ball park by Maryland-National Capital Park and Planning Commission. Mr. Hill loved baseball and he played with the Baltimore Black Sox. He had the opportunity to play with Jackie Robinson, Satchel Paige, Josh Gibson and Roy Campanella. They played games in the Old Griffin Stadium, the present site of Howard University in Washington, D.C.

CLARENCE "PINT" ISRAEL: Born in 1918, this Montgomery County resident grew up playing baseball locally before being asked to tryout for the Washington Royals baseball team. After traveling extensively with the Royals, he was chosen to try out for the Newark Eagles of the Negro National League where he played until called into service for his country. After his tour of duty, "Pint" as he was fondly called, returned to the Eagles where his career culminated in the Eagles beating the Kansas City Monarchs for the 1946 World Series of the Negro League. Years after retiring, "Pint" could still be found teaching youngsters the finer points of the game of baseball, a tradition continued to this day by his son Bobby.

MILTON THOMPSON: Coming from a family of ballplayers, this Montgomery County resident got his start at the age of 8 with the Gaithersburg Sports Association. After standing out in the PeeWee League, "Milt" excelled in football, baseball and track at Magruder High School. While playing with the Damascus American Legion team, he was named "All American" by the Touchdown Club. Milt went on to Howard University where he was drafted by the Atlanta Braves. While with the Philadelphia Phillies in 1993, Milt reached the pinnacle of his career by playing in the World Series. Recently Milt signed with the Los Angeles Dodgers and is currently training for the 1996 season.

PRINCE GEORGES COUNTY

JEREMIAH HAWKINS: Hawkins was from a family of former slaves. In 1920 he became the first Black from Maryland to serve as a delegate to the Republican National Convention. He also became the first mayor of the state's first municipality, North Brentwood.

WILLIAM HENRY, 96
PRESIDENT OF BOWIE STATE FOR 25 YEARS
Dr. Henry was the president of Bowie State form 1942 until 1967. During his tenure, teacher training grew to encompass five buildings. His administration increased the enrollment from 200 students in the Liberal Arts college to 600 students and 15 buildings.

His teaching career started as an elementary teacher in North Carolina. From 1928-1932, he was a Professor of Education and Director of Extension classes at North Carolina Agricultural and Technical State University in Greensboro, N.C.

RAY "SUGAR RAY" LEONARD: After winning the gold medal in the 1976 Olympics, Sugar Ray won five world championships. He won world wide acclaim in heroic battles with Tommie "the Hitman" Hearns, Roberto Duran and Marvelous Marvin Hagler.

CUPID PLUMMER: Cupid earned his and his wife's freedom by fighting in his master's place in the Revolutionary War. His grandson, Adam, was taught to read by a Black Methodist preacher. Adam was a slave for the Calverts.

WILLIAM SIDNEY PITTMAN: A Black architect and son-in-law to Booker T. Washington, Pittman's Black architectural firm became the first to win a federal contract. The contract was to build the $70,000 Negro Building at the National Tricentennial Exposition at Jamestown, Virginia in 1907. He also founded the Fairmount Heights Improvement Company.

JAMES WORMLEY: Wormley operated one of the most successful, elegant hotels in Washington, D.C., located at 15th and H Streets, N.W. Opened in 1871, it had an elevator, telephones, and a heating system.

ST. MARY'S COUNTY

DR. T.J. (THELMA J.) BRYAN: T.J. Bryan is currently the Dean of the Division of Arts and Sciences and the Dean of the Honors Division at Baltimore's Coppin State College. In 1970, she earned a Bachelor of Arts degree in English and speech from Morgan State College, where she was ranked first in her graduating class and where she was inducted into the Alpha Kappa Mu Honor Society. In 1972, she returned to Morgan, where she pursued a Master of Arts degree in English and served as a teaching assistant. In 1974, she entered the doctoral program in English at the University of Maryland at College Park. She earned a Ph.D. in 1982; prior to her graduation, she was inducted into the University of Maryland at College Park chapter of Phi Kappa Phi Honor Society -- the premier honor society at the institution.

That same year, Dr. Bryan was offered a tenure track position as an assistant professor in the Department of Languages, Literature, and Journalism. Presently, she holds the rank of full professor of English.

AGNES KANE CALLUM: An African-American Historian and Author, Ms. Callum graduated from Morgan State College at age 48 and two years later she earned a Master's degree in Social Sciences. Ms. Callum published a Black Genealogical Journal "Flower Of The Forest" and Authored a book "Colored Volunteers Of Maryland - Civil War 7th Regiment U.S. Colored Troops 1836-1866".

Freedom Fighters

TUBBY SMITH: Head Coach of University of Georgia Basketball Team.

MATHIAS DE SOUSA: The first Black man to arrive in Maryland was Mathias de Sousa in 1634. He arrived on the Ark, one of two ships led by Lord Baltimore's brother, Leonard Calvert, at what is known today as Historic St. Mary's City. He was one of nine indentured servants brought to Maryland by Jesuit missionaries. His indenture was finished in 1638 and he became a mariner and fur trader.

SOMERSET COUNTY

LEAH MARY SHELTON: The first person of color to settle in Oriole, Somerset County, Maryland, arriving around 1815 at the age of 21. She was an anomaly of the 1800's. A free Black woman who owned property; she survived a period in which other Blacks were often recaptured and placed back into slavery. Leah took in sewing and hired herself out to clean the houses of neighbors and was able to purchase numerous acres of land. Mrs. Shirley Diggs, wife of Baltimore county historian and author Louis Diggs is a direct descendant of Ms. Shelton.

TALBOT COUNTY

FREDERICK DOUGLASS (1817-1895): Douglass estimated the date of his birth to have been on February 14, 1817 in Tuckahoe, Talbot County. He escaped the horrors of slavery in 1838. For over 50 years Douglass struggled against slavery and the slave trade in America. After teaching himself to read as a slave in Fells Point he became perhaps the greatest orator of his day.

Douglass was the first African-American to meet with a president of the U.S. He published many of his writings; the North Star was his news publication. He was elected president of Black leaders in Washington, DC, President of the Freedman's Bank, Marshal of the District of Columbia, later Recorder of Deeds, named Minister to Haiti, Charge d'affaires for Santo Domingo.

WASHINGTON COUNTY

MARQUERITA & CHARLES DOLEMAN: Mrs. Doleman has been researching and collecting Black History since 1972. She has converted five rooms of her home into the "Doleman Museum".

NATHAN WILLIAMS: Williams was considered the second wealthiest Black in the county. His family owned the property known as Fort Frederick, Maryland for over 50 years before selling it to the Federal Government in 1910.

JAMES W.C. PENNINGTON: James Pennington was born a slave in Washington county in 1809. He was trained as a stone mason and a blacksmith. Pennington escaped slavery in 1830 and received refuge from a Pennsylvania Quaker and was sent to Long Island, New York.

In New York, he studied and eventually became a teacher. James went on to study theology in New Haven, Connecticut, and from 1840 to 1847 was the pastor of the African Congregational Church in Harford, Connecticut.

He became known as a powerful antislavery speaker. After receiving his Doctor of Divinity degree at the University of Heidelburg, he attended congresses at Paris, Brussels, and London. He was often invited to preach and speak before some of the most aristocratic audiences of Europe.

In 1849 his narrative "The Fugitive Blacksmith" was published. He remained a fugitive slave until after the Fugitive Slave Act was passed in 1850; he then purchased his freedom from his former master. Pennington became a prominent leader in the Free Negro Convention Movement. He continued to be a leader in this crusade until his death in 1870.

WICOMICO COUNTY

CHARLES H. & JEANETTE CHIPMAN: Charles served as Principal of Wicomico's county only Black school, for 46 years. The historic John Wesley Methodist Episcopal Church has been restored and renamed the Charles H. Chipman Cultural Center. The church was first built in 1837 by five slaves who had gained their freedom. Mrs. Chipman is a descendant of one of the founders of the church.

MAULANA RON KARENGA: Author and Creator of the celebration of Kwanza, an African-American celebration focusing on the family, community, and culture to refocus African-Americans on the positive aspects of the Black family and community and to counter the negativity associated with blackness. Karenga was born on July 14,

1941 in Parsonsburg, Eastern Shore, Maryland. Books include "The African-American Holiday of Kwanza", Introduction to Black Studies and Kwanza: Origin, Concepts and Justice.

WORCHESTER COUNTY

WILLIAM "JUDY" JOHNSON: (Oct. 26, 1900- June 15, 1989): Judy played in the Negro Leagues from 1923-1937. Judy was the best third baseman of his time and was outstanding as a fielder and an excellent clutch hitter. He batted over .300 most of his career. Johnson helped the Hilldale Daisies win three flags in a row, 1923-24-25.

He also played for the team that is considered the "Best Black Baseball team of all time", the 1935 champion Pittsburgh Crawfords. This all black team featured five future Hall of Famers (Judy Johnson, Joshua Gibson, Oscar Charleston, Satchel Paige, Cool Papa Bell).

Judy Johnson was elected to the National Baseball Hall of Fame in 1974. He was born in Snow Hill, Maryland and spent most of his life as a resident of Wilmington Delaware. On Friday, April 14, 1995 the State of Delaware, the Delaware Stadium Corporation and the City of Wilmington dedicated a eight foot bronze statue of Judy Johnson and renamed the baseball field "The Judy Johnson Field" at Daniel S. Frawley Stadium.

Education

"Destiny is not a matter of chance, it is a matter of choice."

Frederick Douglass

"Let me be fully and clearly understood; I do not come here to reproach Maryland for what happened within her borders in years gone by. Let the dead past bury its dead. I come not to condemn the past but to commend and rejoice over the present.

Even in the gloomiest days of her history, and of my own, I have felt an inexpressible affection for my native state, and hailed with the joy of an exiled son, every indication of progress and civilization she has presented. I have not now, and never had any malice to gratify; I loved Maryland, but hated slavery."

Frederick Douglass
17 November 1864
Bethel Church, Baltimore, MD

FREDERICK DOUGLASS HIGH SCHOOL

Douglass High School is currently located in West Baltimore on Gwynns Falls Parkway. It was established in 1867 as the "Colored Primary School No. 1".

The school received high school status in 1889 and was then called the "Colored High & Grammar School" ...the only Grammar school in the entire city for blacks with grades above fourth. Douglass became the first Colored High School in the entire state of Maryland and remained the only one until 1918. It was also the first colored high school below the Mason-Dixon Line.

THE HISTORY OF CARVER HIGH SCHOOL

George Washington Carver said, "Being a slave was awful, but being uneducated was almost as bad. So I studied hard and finally became a Botanist. I made my reputation by finding all kinds of ways to improve farm productivity. I'm convinced that the seeds of success are in all of us."

The Board of School Commissioners in 1925 authorized the establishment of what is now Carver Vocational-Technical High School as a Colored Vocational School to prepare Negro boys and girls for employment in a trade.

PAUL LAURENCE DUNBAR HIGH SCHOOL

In 1925, the Paul Laurence Dunbar Community High School began serving the residents of East Baltimore. A unique and far-sighted venture began in 1968 when school officials, professional planners and local residents joined together to develop the concept for the $17.5 million mission complex which now occupies several square blocks near the original school.

Education

COPPIN STATE COLLEGE

Dr. Calvin Burnett

From its founding in 1900 to 1963, Coppin was a single-purpose institution designed for the preparation of elementary school teachers. In 1926, the Board of School Commissioners authorized use of the name Fanny Jackson Coppin Normal School, in honor of the great educator who made significant contributions to the education of African-American youth.

CSC, which currently offers 18 programs, including majors in arts and science, education, social work, nursing and criminal justice, draws its strength from many different cultures and background. The 3,540-student population comes from all over the world. Dr. Calvin Burnett has been President of Coppin State since September 1, 1970.

MORGAN STATE UNIVERSITY

Dr. Earl Richardson

Established in 1867, when many black institutions came into being under the Freedman's Bureau. Noted for its Beulah M. Davis Special Collections Room in the Sopher Library are artifacts and memorabilia of Frederick Douglass, Matthew Henson, Benjamin Banneker and other famous Blacks from Maryland. A particularly outstanding statute of Douglass by Black sculptor James Lewis graces the center of the campus. The Murphy Fine Arts Gallery offers continually changing exhibits by black artists. Located at Hillen Road and Coldspring Lane, Baltimore, the gallery and library are open Monday to Friday during school hours.

SOJOURNER DOUGLASS COLLEGE

Dr. Charles Simmons

Dr. Charles W. Simmons is President and founder of Sojourner Douglass College, Baltimore, Maryland. A native of Baltimore, he is a graduate of the Union Graduate School where he earned his Ph.D in Administration of Higher Education in 1978. The college is named after Sojourner Truth and Frederick Douglass. A three year degree course is offered.

Other Historically Black Colleges in the State of Maryland are: University of Maryland Eastern Shore and Bowie State University.

Sam Lacy, Mayor Kurt Schmoke and Buck O'Neil

MARYLAND
AFRICAN-AMERICANS IN SPORTS

The State of Maryland has a great sports history and African-Americans have greatly contributed to this legacy.

BASEBALL
NEGRO LEAGUES
BLACK BASEBALL IN BALTIMORE

BALTIMORE BLACK SOX

Duration
1916-34

Honors: League pennants ('29, '32)
Affiliations: ECL ('23-'28), ANL ('29), EWL ('32)
Independent ('16-'22, '30-'31), NNL ('33-'34)

The Black Sox started as an independent team in 1916 but was clearly not of major-league caliber at the onset. After becoming charter members of the league, the Black Sox fielded strong teams each season, but a pennant always eluded them. The Black Sox won the pennant in 1929, the league's only year of existence, with a composite mark of 49-21 for the year.

Rap Dixon, Satchel Paige, Biz Mackey, Laymon Yokely and Hall of Famer Leon Day played with the Black Sox. Vincent Lee played short stop for the Black Sox in 1933 and he currently resides in Baltimore.

BALTIMORE ELITE GIANTS

From Columbus, Ohio (1935) to Washington, D.C. (1936-37) the Elites found their home in Baltimore in 1938.

The ballclub remained a fixture in the city for the next thirteen years. During the Elites' years in the Negro National League, the Homestead Grays was the dominant team, claiming nine consecutive titles, and competition was fierce between the two teams. The Elites battled them every year for league supremacy, and in 1939 the Elites claimed a championship when they defeated the Grays in a four-team post season tournament.

In 1949, the Elites won both halves of the split season to capture the Eastern Division title, and swept the Western Division's Chicago American Giants in four straight games to claim the league championship.

Jim Gilliam, Joe Black and Roy Campanella started their careers with the Elite Giants prior to joining the Brooklyn Dodgers. Former Elite Giants, Ernest Burke, Vincent Lee and Bert Simmons still reside in the Baltimore area. Hall of Famer Leon Day played on the 1949 Championship Team, along with Bill Byrd, Frazier Robinson and the late Al "Apples" Wilmore.

BALTIMORE ELITE GIANTS 1949

LEON DAY

Leon Day was the greatest pitcher in the last 15 years of the Negro Leagues. Day played baseball for 22 years beginning on the sandlots of Mt. Winans in West Baltimore, going to six countries and finally to the hallowed halls of Cooperstown, New York — home of the National Baseball Hall of Fame.

Leon Day was born on October 30, 1916. Leon holds the single game strikeout record for the Negro Leagues (19) and also holds the season strikeout record in Puerto Rico.

Day won five (5) championships (Mexico, Valenzula, 1944 GI World Series, 1946 Newark Eagles, 1949 Baltimore Elite Giants). He played in 7 Negro Leagues East-West All Star Games; outdueled the legendary Satchel Paige three out of four games; and was elected to three Hall of Fames. Newark Sports Hall of Fame, Puerto Rico Professional Baseball of Fame and on July 30, 1995 Day was officially inducted into the Major League National Baseball Hall of Fame.

In July 1995, Mayor Kurt L. Schmoke renamed the Eutaw Street entrance in front of Oriole Park at Camden Yards "THE LEON DAY WAY". His sister, Mrs. Ida M. Bolden remarked how fitting it was because the entrance is adjacent to the remodeled Camden Street Station - where she and Leon arrived in Baltimore in 1916.

BALTIMORE ORIOLES

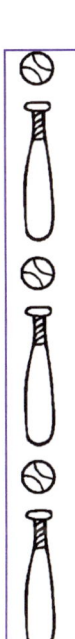

Elrod Hendricks joined the Orioles in 1968 as a catcher and today, some 28 years later, Elrod is serving as a coach.

Acknowledged as one of the best players ever to play baseball, Frank Robinson is the first African-American to be a manager in major league baseball. Robinson is the only player ever to hit a ball out of Memorial Stadium

In 1983, future Hall of Famer & 500 home run hitter, Eddie Murray teamed with a young shortstop named Cal Ripken, Jr. to lead the O's to their third World Series championship.

Lee May, Paul Blair, Curt Morton, Don Buford, Ken Singleton, Al Bumbry, and Reggie Jackson were Orioles.

Clifford "Connie" Johnson, a teammate of the legendary Satchel Paige on the Negro League Kansas City Monarchs, remains the only Black man to start and pitch an opening day game for the Orioles. Connie would pitch eight major league shutouts.

500 HOME RUN HITTERS CLUB

NAME	# HOME RUNS	HISTORICAL DATE
Hank Aaron	755	July 14, 1968
Babe Ruth	714	August 11, 1929
Willie Mays	660	Sept. 13, 1965
Frank Robinson	**586**	**Sept. 13, 1971**
Harmon Killebrew	573	August 10, 1971
Mike Schmidt	563	April 18, 1987
Reggie Jackson	**563**	**Sept 17, 1984**
Willie McCovey	563	June 30, 1978
Mickey Mantle	536	May 14, 1967
Jimmie Foxx	534	Sept 24, 1940
Ted Williams	521	June 17, 1960
Ernie Banks	512	May 12, 1970
Eddie Matthew	512	July 14, 1967
Eddie Murray	**500**	**September 6, 1996**
Mel Ott	511	August 1, 1945

Sports

EDDIE MURRAY

Eddie Murray is one of the Orioles and baseball's greatest players. In 1996, after 20 years in the Majors, Eddie began the third player in history to have over 3000 hits and 500 homeruns. His 19 grand slams places him second behind Lou Gerhig's 23. He is second in double plays, third in putouts and has won three Gold Glove awards. His 1,874 RBI's is 8th all-time. EDDIE! EDDIE! EDDIE! A future Hall of Famer.

FRANK ROBINSON

Frank's achievements during his 21 seasons as a player rank him among the top players of all-time in 10 categories. His 586 home runs places him 4th on the all-time homerun list.

The trade that brought Frank from Cincinnati to Baltimore turned the Orioles from contenders to World Champions in 1966. He won the Triple Crown (316 batting average, 49 homers, 122 RBI) and was both the American League and World Series MVP in his first season with the Orioles. In all, the Orioles went to the World Series 4 times in his 6 seasons as a player with them. When he was traded to the Dodgers after the '71 season, he became the first player to have his number retired by the Orioles.

Frank was N.L. Rookie of the Year with the Reds in 1956 and is the only player to win MVP honors in both leagues ('61 N.L., '66 A.L.) He played in 11 All-Star games and was MVP of the 1971 classic. While still an active player, he became the first black manager in major league history with the Cleveland Indians in 1975. He later managed the San Francisco Giants and the Orioles. He spent 19 seasons with the Orioles as a player, coach ('79-'80 and '85-'87), manager ('88-'91) and assistant general manager ('91-'95). Elected to baseball's Hall of Fame the first year he was eligible in 1982. Frank lives with his wife, Barbara, in Bel Air, CA. They have two children.

Basketball

Basketball Heroes

The greatest high school basketball teams of all times have laced up at the school known as DUNBAR HIGH SCHOOL in Baltimore, MD. The Dunbar Poets have a history of winning state championships in basketball and football.

Former Dunbar Coach Bob Wade led a team of future NBA players to National championships; his team included the late Reggie Lewis, Tyrone "Mugsy" Bogues, David Wingate and Reggie Williams.

Another Dunbar graduate Sam Cassell has won two NBA Championships with the Houston Rockets. Dante Bright, Kwame Evans and Keith Booth are former Dunbar High standouts who are now playing on the collegiate level.

Other Baltimoreans starring in basketball were Marvin Webster, Patrick McKinney, Len Bias, Skip Wise and Ernie Graham.

But also there is Southern High, Lake Clifton and DeMatha High where basketball legends are groomed for future roles in the NBA.

Coppin State College:

Maryland's most successful college basketball teams hail from center city Baltimore - none other than the Coppin State Eagles. Coach Ron "Fang" Mitchell and the Eagles captured the MEAC title in 1990, 1993 and again in 1997. The women's team won their MEAC title in 1991.

MEAC Champs - 1991

Terquin Mott, Antoine Brockington, Reggie Welch, Reggie Isaac, Phil Booth, Shelton and Larry Stewart (NBA) all played under Coach Ron "Fang" Mitchell. Fang's Eagles became the first team from the MEAC to win a first round game in the NCAA Division I Tournament.

James Mosher Little League Team - 1996

UNIVERSITY OF MARYLAND - COLLEGE PARK:
Keith Booth, Rodney Elliott, Laron Profit, Joe Smith, Buck Williams, Len Bias, John Lucas, Len Elmore, Albert King, Ernie Graham, Tony Massenberg

PROFESSIONAL BASKETBALL

Baltimore Bullets
Gus "Honeycomb" Johnson, Wes Unseld, Earl "the Pearl" Monroe, The Big "E" Elvin Hayes, Phil Chenier.

Wes Unseld played center on the 1971 NBA Champions Washington Bullets team. Unseld is one of only two NBA players to be voted "Most Valuable Player" and "Rookie of the Year" in his first season in the pros. Unseld, Hayes, Johnson, are the only bullets to have their jersey retired.

BOXING

Joe Gans, a lightweight boxer from Baltimore city, became Maryland's first world champion in the sport of boxing (1901-1908).

Sugar Ray Leonard of Palmer Park, MD (Prince George's County) won a Gold Medal at the 1976 Olympics and won World Boxing championships in five different weight classes.

Baltimore's Vincent Pettaway won a middleweight boxing championship in 1995.

Mack Lewis a veteran boxing trainer operates a gym in Baltimore for aspiring boxers.

FOOTBALL

City College
He was the lacrosse midfielder and the quarterback, leading City College to four straight football titles. He would continue his heroics in the arena of higher learning at Yale, Oxford, Harvard, a Rhodes Scholar and now into his third term as Mayor of Baltimore City - Mayor Kurt L. Schmoke.

Morgan State University
COACH EARL C. "PAPA BEAR" BANKS: Earl C. Banks, former head coach and athletic director, coached the Morgan Bears during the team's 31-game winning streak and three unbeaten seasons, five Central Intercollegiate Athletic Conference titles, and two consecutive victories in national bowl competitions; Orange Blossom Classic,

Sports

1965, against Florida A&M; and Tangerine Bowl, against West Chester State.

Recognized as one of the leading football coaches in the nation during this 25 years at Morgan, Coach Earl C. Banks had an astonishing legacy which includes numerous young men who became successful professional football players including:

Willie Lanier, Kansas City Chiefs	James Phillips, Winnipeg Bombers
Leroy Kelly, Cleveland Browns	Ray Chester, Baltimore Colts
George Nock, Washington Redskins	Mark Washington, Dallas Cowboys
John Fuqua, Pittsburgh Steelers	Willie Germany, Philadelphia Eagles

Stump Mitchell, former NFL running back is Head Coach at MSU.

Coach Phillips - Under Coach Phillips, Morgan State University has won ten straight MEAC wrestling championships.

Baltimore Colts:
Calvin Hill, John Mackey, Lenny Moore and Jim Parker are former Baltimore Colts who have been inducted into the Pro Football Hall of Fame. Lydell Mitchell, Eugene "Big Daddy" Lipscomb, Joe Washington, Glen "Shake & Bake" Doughtery were great athletes in the heyday of the Baltimore Colts.

Martial Arts

Lynette Love of Charles County was an Olympic gold medalist in Tae Kwon Doe. Leroy Taylor & Eddie Butcher of Baltimore are champions in full contact Karate. Riley Hawkins, a Master Teacher.

Sports Writer

SAM LACY at age 93 is still covering sports for the Baltimore African-American Newspaper. His sports writing career began over seventy years ago at the Washington Afro-American Newspaper. Sam is a member of the Black Journalist Hall of Fame, and the first African-American to join the Baseball Writers of America Association.

Track

Ron Freeman of Coppin State College won a gold medal at the 1966 Olympics. Freeman carried the Olympic Torch for the 1996 Olympics. Rochelle Stevens of Morgan State University, won a gold medal as a member of the 1996 Olympic women's 4x400 meter relay team. From 1984-88, Ms Stevens was named to 11 All-American teams, and was Division I 400 meter champion. She was honored as Morgan's Most Valuable Athlete and holds the school record for the 100, 200, and 400 meters.

Sports

A Special Tribute to Jackie Robinson

50th Anniversary of Breaking the Color Barrier
1947-1997

JACKIE ROBINSON 50th ANNIVERSARY AWARDS BANQUET

42 — Guest Speaker - Ms. Sharon Robinson — 42

Honorees
SAM LACY
DON NEWCOMBE
REX BARNEY
JOE BLACK
LENNY MOORE

Friday, April 18, 1997
7:00pm-11:00pm

Renaissance Hotel
201 E. Pratt Street
Baltimore, MD

SPECIAL TRIBUTE
NEGRO LEAGUES BASEBALL PLAYERS

sponsored by Baltimore African-American Tourism Council, WJZ-13, Afro-American Newspapers, WBAL, Radio One, National Alliance of African-American Athletes, Steven Pace Co, Baltimore Bicentennial Celebration, Inc.

"Applause for Dawes"

Dominique Dawes qualified for the 1996 summer Olympics in Atlanta. She led the U.S. team to win a Bronze Medal at the 1992 Olympic games in Barcelona. In 1994 she won the all around National Championships and all four individual events - the first gymnast to accomplish that in 25 years. Dawes parents enrolled her in a gymnastics class at age six. Dawes a straight "A" student is from Takoma Park, Maryland and plans to attend Stanford University. During the 1996 Summer Olympics, Dominique's high scores helped lead the U.S. Gymnastic team to a Gold Medal. Dawes also captured a Bronze Medal in the floor exercise.

DAWES' RECORD

1992: World Championships, 16th in vault; Olympics, 26th all-around.

1993: National Championships, 2nd all-around, 1st vault; World Championships, 4th all-around, 2nd uneven bars and balance beam.

1994: American Cup, 1st all-around, swept event finals; World Championships, 5th all-around; National Championships, 1st all-around, swept event finals; World Team Trials, 1st all-around.

1995: World Team Championships, 2nd; National Championships, 4th all-around, 1st uneven bars and floor exercise; World Team Trials, 5th all-around (injured for World Championships).

1996: National Championships, 4th all-around, swept event finals; Olympic Trials, 3rd all-around.

1996: Gold and Bronze Olympic Medal Winner — Centennial Olympic Games

Pastor REV. DR. JOHN L. WRIGHT

First Baptist Church of Guilford

1996 Theme:
"Teaching, Preaching & Healing"
Matthew 4:23

SUNDAY MORNING WORSHIP
8:00 a.m. and 11:00 a.m.

SUNDAY SCHOOL
9:15 a.m.

MONDAY THRU THURSDAY
Senior Citizens - 10:00 a.m.

Men/Boys Tutorial - 6:30 p.m.
(Mondays only)

Walk Through The Bible
(E.B.S.)
7:00 p.m.

Winning Souls for Christ!

Rejoice

FRIDAY
Boys Scout Troop #513
6:30 p.m.

7504 Oakland Mills Road ◆ Columbia, Maryland 21046
410-792-7096

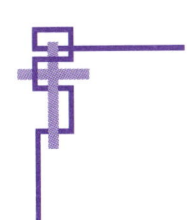

Happy 50th Anniversary

Full Gospel Baptist Church
June 30-1946 - June 30, 1996

"The End of Your Search for a Caring Church"

We invite you to visit the
FULL GOSPEL BAPTIST CHURCH AND MUSEUM

Pastor Reverend James H. Stovall, Sr.
FULL GOSPEL BAPTIST CHURCH
14340 Frederick Road † Cooksville, MD 21723
Church Phone: 410-489-5069

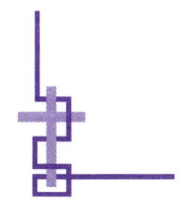

Founders:
Reverend John Wesley Holland
Reverend William and Lydia Adams

Israel Baptist Church Of Baltimore City

The Church Where "Everybody is Somebody"

BIBLE TEACHING ◆ MISSION TRAINING
PRAYER SERVICE ◆ TAPE MINISTRY
SUNDAY CHURCH SCHOOL
MEN'S MINISTRY BIBLE STUDY
WOMEN MINISTRY BIBLE STUDY
NAACP YOUTH COUNCIL MEETING
SUBSTANCE ABUSE MINISTRY
HIV SUPPORT GROUP MEETING
THE "SANCTUARY WITHOUT WALLS"

Going beyond the walls of the sanctuary to reach out to those in the community without a Church Home

SUNDAY SERVICES:
7:45am & 11:00am Morning Worship ▪ 9:30am Sunday School
Radio Ministry - 10:00am on Heaven 600

Committed to Glorifying God and Edifying Man

PASTOR H. WALDEN WILSON, II
1220 N. Chester Street ◆ Baltimore, MD 21213
410-732-3494 Church Office ◆ 410-732-1516 Pastor's Office

Timothy Baptist Church
"Church With A Vision"
1214-16 W. Saratoga Street
Baltimore, Maryland 21223
James L. Ball, Minister

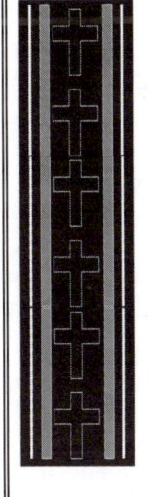

Christian's Brotherhood

Seniors' Fellowship Group

Quarterly Prayer Breakfast

Twelve Step Program

Educational Enrichment Center

Young Women's Christian Fellowship

Sunday School
9:30 a.m.

Morning Worship
11:00 a.m.

Telephone:
Church: (410) 728-1447/481-1111
Pastor's Study: (410) 383-0901
Fax: (410) 383-7324

Bible Class
Prayer Service
Fridays
7:00 p.m.

Communion
4th Sunday

THE STEVEN PACE UPHOLSTERING CO. INC.
Home of Pace Galleries

WE ARE THE UPHOLSTERS FOR MARYLAND'S LEADING DESIGNERS

- Reupholstering and Refinishing
- Antique Restoration
- Rush Bottoms
- Cushions Refilled
- Caning and Wicker Repair
- We Also Manufacture to Order
- No Job Too Big or Too Small!
- Dining Room Chairs Reglued & Repaired

Thanks to You We Are Growing!

Visit Our Workroom and See Our Skilled Craftsmen at Work!

FREE Estimates, Pick-up & Delivery

10% OFF
All Labor
to Senior Citizens

The Steven Pace Upholstering Co. Inc.
727-729-B Frederick Rd. • Catonsville, MD 21228

Member of Catonsville Chamber of Commerce

CALL

410-744-0640
The House that Quality Built

25% OFF
All Fabrics

The Steven Pace Upholstering Co. Inc.

BALTIMORE - WHERE BLACK HERITAGE BEGINS - 90

AFRICAN-AMERICAN BUSINESSES & SERVICES DIRECTORY

INFORMATION HOTLINE - 410-783-5469

BALTIMORE CITY AND BALTIMORE COUNTY
(use area code 410)

ACCOUNTANT
Abrams, Foster, Noble & Williams ◆ Village of Cross Keys 433-6830
Collins & Associates ◆ 4 W. Bend Ct. 281-1269/847-5688
Alagra McClendon 233-7275
Joan Pratt, CPA & Associates ◆ 1532 Havenwood Rd., #204 243-1200
Bruce Royster, CPA ◆ 2901 Druid Park Dr. 669-6033
Wilkins McNair ◆ 201 N. Charles St. .... 962-5252/244-0753*(fax)*

ACTOR/ACTRESS
Browne, Andre T. 783-8214
Day, Verna Lee 448-9268

ADMINISTRATIVE SERVICES
Fine Points 433-6843

ADOPTION SERVICES
Family & Children's Services of Central Maryland 669-9000

ADVERTISING
African-American Resource & Tourist Guide 783-5469
AM Communications. 601-0230

ADVERTISING SPECIALTIES
Positive Publications Printing & Products Co. 607-4941
Speciality Marketing & Printing ◆ 9008 Liberty Rd. 922-1233
The Thank You Shoppe ◆ 6000 Harford Rd. 426-6222

AFRICAN FASHIONS
African-American Fashions◆ 7031 Liberty Rd. 281-1310
Authentic Afrikan Fabric◆ 1335 Hickory Springs Cr. 788-5972
Everyone's Place ◆ 1356 W. North Ave. 728-0877
Expressions Cultural Center ◆ 222 N. Paca St. 783-0195
Out of Africa ◆ 111 W. Saratoga St. 752-5808

QUESTION:
Name the First Bank

BLACK FACT

Freedmen's Savings Bank

African-American Businesses & Services

EVERYONE'S PLACE

AFRICAN CULTURAL CENTER
Bookstore - African Village
Art, Fashions & Accessories

1356 W. NORTH AVE.
BALTIMORE, MARYLAND 21217
(410) 728-0877

ALARM SYSTEMS
Safeguard Enterprises, Inc. 590-3036

AMBULANCE SERVICES
T.L.C. Ambulance Service 922-7600

ANIMAL SERVICES
Ammons Animal Hospital ♦ 4901 Liberty Heights Ave. 542-3308

ANTIQUE DEALERS & SHOPS
LaPetite Collection (Egyptian & Moroccan) ♦ 2429 St. Paul St. 662-1886
Steven Pace ♦ 727-729 Frederick Rd. 744-0622

WATCH FOR THE
GRAND OPENING   GRAND OPENING

THE PACE GALLERY
A Division of the Steven Pace Co.
727-729 Frederick Rd. • Catonsville, MD 21228
410-744-0640
Antiques • Consignments • Furniture
Art Memorabilia Estate • Purchasing

WE BUY AND SELL ANTIQUES
✷ Consignments By Appointment   ✷ Auction Room

ARCHITECTS
TLC/Leon Bridges ♦ 805 E. Fayette St. 659-0200
J.V. Lee ♦ 1401 Northgate Rd. 323-0053
Christopher Amadi 335-9555

African-American Businesses & Services

ART SALES/GALLERIES
Aware 947-7667
Black American Museum ♦ 1769 Carswell St. 243-9600
Black Heritage Art, Inc. ♦ 9810½ Liberty Rd., Randallstown 389-0967
Cultural Gallery of Fine Art ♦ .... 381-1199/750-3292 *(fax)*
    7282 Cradlerock Way, Columbia, MD
Shades of Beauty ♦ 6901 Security Blvd., Security Square Mall 944-4327
Eulipion Art Gallery♦ 2442 N. Charles St. 235-3922
Expressions Cultural Center ♦ 222 Paca St. 783-0195
Family Tree ♦ 825 E. Baltimore St. 576-0880
Personal Preference Inc. (Jammy Jones) 602-0849

ARTISTS
Herb of Eden Co., Inc. - Bey Bey Williams 563-1798
Hiawatha Howard ♦ 3800 W. Coldspring Lane 367-5111
Roberts Images ♦ 2725 Walbrook Ave. 383-7056

ASSOCIATIONS
African-American Business Association 727-1119
Alliance of Black Women Attorneys 377-1019
Baltimore Association of Black Media Workers 547-6705
The Business League of Baltimore, Inc. ♦ 2901 Druid Park Dr. 728-7481
The Hub ♦ 2901 Druid Park Dr., Ste 209 669-1888
The Monumental City Bar Association 889-4200
NAACP ♦ 4805 Mt. Hope Dr. 358-8900

AUTO ACCESSORIES
Frank R. Epps Co., Inc. .... 301-336-7855/336-0747(fax)
    101 Maryland Park Drive ♦ Capitol Heights, MD

AUTO REPAIR
Dixon Auto Repair & Paint Shop ♦ 2340 Belair Rd. 327-4342
Everything Automotive, Inc. ♦ 2600 Gwynns Falls Pkwy 462-0920
Johnson's Automotive ♦ 4821 Windsor Mill Rd. 448-1565
Northwest Body & Fender, Inc. ♦ 4924 Reisterstown Rd. 664-7776

BAIL BONDS
Campbell's Brothers Bail Bonds .... 225-3111 or 523-2489
Cody Smith Bail Bond ♦ 2409 Reisterstown Rd. 462-2639
Robinson Bail Bond ♦ 2110 N. Calvert St. 234-0108/234-0104

BAKERIES
B&D Edibles ♦ 3116 Greenmead Rd. 521-8520
Edith Bennett *(Specializing in Wedding Cakes)* 235-9547
Crazy Cakes *by Jenifer D.* 882-2370
Salaam Bakery ♦ 5455 Park Heights Ave. 542-8202

African-American Businesses & Services

Supreme Oasis Bakery & Deli ♦ 3221 Garrison Blvd. 466-7212
Truly Scratch ♦ 1041 W. Baltimore St. 547-7674

BALLOONS
Balloon Decorator *(Jeveta Jones)* 254-0966
Bundles of Joy ♦ Westside Shopping Ctr., 2400 Frederick Ave. 233-4355
DOZ Flowers & Balloons ♦ 3412 Greenmount Ave. 235-6773
Thank You Shoppe ♦ 6000 Harford Rd. 426-6222

BANKS
Advance Federal Savings & Loan - 3 Locations
   1405 E. Coldspring Lane. 323-9570
   1611 W. North Ave. 523-7100
   3411 Clifton Ave. 233-6570
Harbor Bank - 6 Locations
   25 W. Fayette St. 528-1801
   5000 Park Heights Ave. 367-3331
   5109 York Rd. 433-3993
   3240 Erdman Ave. 675-1167
   8600 Liberty Rd. 521-8600
   6812 Riverdale Rd., Riverdale, MD 301-577-5100

BANQUET/SPECIAL EVENTS/RECEPTION FACILITIES
Baltimore Grand ♦ 401 W. Fayette St. 385-4100
Forum Caterers ♦ 4210 Primrose Ave. 358-1101
Gallery of Events ♦ 429 N. Eutaw St. 783-1846
The Forest ♦ 214 Cedar Lane, Glen Burnie, MD 789-3553
Nixon's Farm ♦ 2800 Rte. 32, West Friendship, MD 21794 442-2151

BARBERSHOPS
The Detailer ♦ 5900 York Rd., Ste. 203 435-1330
Edmondson Village Barbershop ♦ 4506 Edmondson Ave. 947-2233
Lenny's House of Naturals ♦ 1099 W. Fayette St. 727-9123

BEAUTY SALONS & SUPPLIES
Imani Hair Braiding & Weaving Salon ♦ 427 N. Eutaw St. 385-1369
Short Cutz ♦ 330 N. Paca St. 783-1378
A Perfect 10 Hair Salon ♦ 500 W. Franklin St. 523-9898
Manley's Barber Shop ♦ 224 Park Ave. 752-2833
Phaze Uno Hair ♦ 206 W. Saratoga St. 625-2232
Cut-Up & Company ♦ 411 Park Ave. 685-2866
Mane Attraction Hair Salon ♦ 119 W. Mulberry St. 837-8221
Stephanie's Hair Care ♦ 227 W. Mulberry St. 727-9268

African-American Businesses & Services

BILLING SERVICES
Comedent Consultants ♦ 6814 Sauter Lane 944-2993

COMEDENT CONSULTANTS

**Electronic Billing Service
Computer Software
Office Automation**

SHEILA HALL CDA, MT
Office: 410-944-2993   Fax: 410-944-4770

BOOK STORES
Afrikan World Books 383-0511
Cover To Cover Book Store Cafe, ... 410-381-9200/381-9201 *(fax)*
    7284 Cradlerock Way, Columbia, MD 21045
Cultural Eye Production ♦ 3210 Howard Park Ave. 448-3423
Everyone's Place ♦ 1356 W. North Ave. 728-0877
Expression's Cultural Center ♦ 222 N. Paca St. 783-0195
Family Health Education Service (Heritage Bible, Stories for Children) 433-0272
House of Wisdom Book Center ♦ 2313 W. Lafayette St. 945-8429
Jesus Shops ♦ Mondawmin Mall 728-3364
NorthStar Bookstore ♦ 7025 Liberty Rd. 265-8787
Pyramid Books ♦ Mondawmin Mall 383-8800
Shades of Beauty ♦ Security Square Mall 944-4327
Upward Way Church Supply ♦ 459 Old Town Mall 962-5333

BUS COMPANIES
Boykin Transportation ♦ 4015-17 Ken Oak Ave. 358-4549
Eatman's Transportation ♦ 2552 Woodbrook Ave. 462-4493
Ferguson's Chartered Bus Co. ♦ 46 S. Franklintown Rd. 945-9000
H.B. Tour & Travel, Inc. ♦ 5504 Chandler Ave. 448-0460
Gladney Charter Bus ♦ 2301 Sinclair Lane 522-4900
Johnson's Transportation ♦ 3200 Reisterstown Rd. 664-5236
M.R. Hopkins ♦ 2600 Presstman St. 362-2984
Midway Charter ♦ 2601 Baker St. 624-7820
Parran Bus Line ♦ 300 S. Ellamont St. 947-0771

BUSINESS OPPORTUNITIES
Excel Telecommunications 347-1430
    P.O. Box 22167, 21203 - Mildred Hawkins, Independent Rep.
Kaire International 581-3626

Now 6 Friendly, Convenient Professional Offices

MEETING THE NEEDS OF THE COMMUNITY

THE HARBOR BANK OF MARYLAND

MAIN OFFICE
25 West Fayette Street
(410) 528-1801

PIMLICO OFFICE
5000 Park Heights Avenue
(410) 367-3331

YORK ROAD OFFICE
5109 York Road
(410) 433-3993

RIVERDALE OFFICE
6812 Riverdale Road
(301) 577-5100

ERDMAN OFFICE
3240 Belair Road
(410) 675-1167

RANDALLSTOWN OFFICE
8600 Liberty Road
410) 521-8600

EACH DEPOSITOR INSURED TO $100,000 BY FDIC

• Member FDIC • Equal Opportunity Lender • Equal Housing Opportunity

African-American Businesses & Services

Big Breaks for Small Business

That's why minority-owned businesses are moving to Maryland from all over America.

Like other business people, you have plans and dreams.

But if you're starting a small business in today's economic climate, you will also have problems. That's where the State of Maryland fits into your scheme of things.

In Maryland, problems which face minority-owned businesses are understood — and overcome. Our four-point Minority Business Financing Program is a model, nationwide. The program is designed to get your business started. And keep it growing.

We offer service in these four important areas:

- Contract Financing
- Long-Term Loan Guaranties
- Surety Bonds and Bond Guaranties
- Equity Investments for Franchises, Business Acquisitions and Technology-Based Businesses

We also offer continuous educational workshops and conferences to enhance the financial and management skills of minority business entrepreneurs.

To discover where you fit into Maryland's business picture, phone us today.

Maryland Small Business Development Financing Authority (MSBDFA) (410) 333-4270

Maryland
Department of Business & Economic Development

African-American Businesses & Services

BUSINESS SERVICES

African-American Business Association-Baltimore City 727-1119
Allen Professional Group ♦ 9904 Cervidae Lane, #3 521-8091
Certification Program - Baltimore 396-3424
City Chamber of Commerce 837-7102
    204 E. Lombard St., 3rd Fl., Herget Harbor Building
Baltimore County Chamber of Commerce 825-6200
Baltimore Economic Opportunity ♦ 800 N. Charles St. 576-2326
Development Credit Fund, Inc. ♦ 2530 N. Charles St., Ste 200 467-7500
MSBDFA Management Group, Inc. ♦ 217 E. Redwood St. 659-7850
MD Small Business Development Financing Authority 333-4270
MD/DC Minority Supplier Development Council.......................... 997-7588
State Certification Program - MD State Dept. of Transp. 859-7327
Small Business Administration ♦ 10 N. Calvert St., 10th Fl. 962-3218
Small Business Resource Center ♦ 3 W. Baltimore St..................... 605-0900

CAB COMPANY
ABC Cab Co. 323-4222

CAR REPAIR
Everything Automotive, Inc. ♦ 2600 Gwynns Falls Parkway 462-0920
Genesis Auto Repair ♦ 5205 Eleanora Ave. 466-3605

CAR WASH
Car Care Center ♦ North Ave. & McCullough St............................
Downtown Hand Car Wash ♦ 405 W. Monument St. 523-7882

CARPET - SALES & CLEANING
Carpet City Distributors ♦ 4662 York Rd. 323-7001
DuraClean.. 444-7247

CATERERS
Ashby Food Services 662-9383
Baltimore Grand ♦ 401 W. Fayette St. 385-4101
Catering For All Occasions 362-2396
C'est Cheese ♦ 400 W. Lexington St. 659-5541
Class Act Caterers ♦ 628 N. Chester St. 732-8880
Culinary Innovations ♦ 2118 Maryland Ave.................................. 234-0330
Do-Re Mi Catering ♦ P.O. Box 4535, 21212......................... 906-9717
Forum Caterers ♦ 4210 Primrose Ave.. 358-1101
Shoe Box Lunches 727-0755
Special Occasions ♦ 6414 Reisterstown Rd. 358-9300
Twins Catering ♦ 1016 S. Charles St. 547-2636

CERAMICS
Frances Ceramics ♦ 4003 Frederick Rd. 242-6045

African-American Businesses & Services

CHARITIES
Associated Black Charities ♦ 1114 Cathedral St. 659-0000
CHECK CASHING
Star & Crescent Check Cashing ♦ 3317 Garrison Blvd. 542-2750
CHILD CARE
Ashburton Day Nursery ♦ 3050 Liberty Hgts Ave. 664-8393
Good News Children Daycare ♦ 600 W. North Ave. 728-0652
Kiddie Castle Child Development Center, Inc. 542-4949
Loving Care Day Nursery ♦ 1306A Gorsuch Ave. 467-7335
New Era Daycare/St. Bernadine's Church-3812 Edmondson Ave. ... 233-5100
Shelia's Stay & Play Daycare ♦ 1829 W. Mulberry St. 945-5871
CHILDREN STORE
Wee-Folks 664-3104

WEE FOLKS

Unique Specialty Toys, Gifts and Educational Playthings
CALL 410-664-3104 to get on mailing list.
Check our web site: http://www.active.weefolks
Send e-mail: greatgif@ix.netcom.com

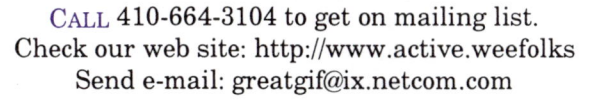

CLEANERS
Aljay One Hour Cleaning ♦ 2800 W. North Ave. 462-9830
Destiny Dry Cleaning & Laundry Service ♦ 3843 Crestlyn Rd. 467-1300
Sparky One Hour Cleaners ♦ 4721 Liberty Heights Ave. 542-2000
Quality Tailoring ♦ 5 Light St., Ste. 110 685-6414

JAMES E. WHITE
President

QUALITY TAILORING INC.
Ladie's and Men's Custom Clothing and Alterations

5 Light Street, Suite 110 • Baltimore, Maryland 21202
410-685-6414   Fax 685-2220

African-American Businesses & Services

COLLEGES
Coppin State College ♦ 2500 W. North Ave. 383-5926
Morgan State University ♦ Coldspring Lane & Hillen Rd. 319-3022
Sojourner-Douglass College ♦ 501 N. Caroline St. 276-0306

COMMERCIAL/VIDEO PRODUCTION
R. Johnson 356-6906

COMPUTER SALES & SERVICES
Best Buy Computer ♦ Melvin Warren 669-4323
Brown's Engineering Inc. ♦ 5217 York Rd., Ste. 102 ...... 323-5644/323-5645
ECS Technologies, Inc. ♦ 1530 Caton Center Dr. ...... 242-2200/242-0922*(fax)*
Genesis Micro-World Computer Services 655-6009
Genesis Office Systems ♦ 940 Madison Ave. 225-0500
Second Byte ♦ 1114 Reisterstown Rd. 653-2052
System Configuration & Maintenance Corp. ♦ 701 W. Osten St. .. 727-1119

Brown's Engineering, Inc.
Specializing in hardware, software, LAN Sales and Service of Computer Systems

5127 YORK RD., BALTIMORE, MD 21212
Tel: 323-5644/323-5645 (fax)
Pager 813-8144
Office: 1-800-546-9300

CONFERENCE AND SPECIAL EVENT PLANNING
Allen Professional Group 521-8091
Heart II Soul Productions 244-1436
Professional Conference Services. .... 669-0208/669-0679 *(fax)*
     2319 N.Eutaw Place, Suite #2 ♦ email: pbrice@crosslink.net
Pro-Baltimore ♦ 1322 Eutaw St., Ste. 2R .... 462-1285/462-3259*(fax)*
Ty Johnson Special Events Management & Consulting 909-2417

We Care at . . .
CAMPBELL'S CORNER
LELA BLUE -- President

"Offering insurance of all kinds to meet your needs and pocket."

- Life/Health
- Bailbonds
- Renters
- Homeowner
- Business
- Fire
- Notary
- Automobile
- Insurance Classes Offered

(410) 225 - 3111
Fax: (410) 225 - 9746

800 N.Fulton Ave.-- 2nd fl.
Baltimore, MD 21217

African-American Businesses & Services

Francine Allen, President

Allen Professional Group

DO YOU NEED SOMEONE TO:

Motivate Your Staff
Train Your Employees
Coordinate that Special Event

Allen Professional Group Does All That *and More!*

*Meeting your
training and motivational needs
with a professional and personal touch!*

PROFESSIONAL CLIENTS INCLUDE:
Downtown Partnership of Baltimore ♦ V103/Heaven 600
For Sisters Only Expo ♦ Black Professional Men of MD
MD Historically Black Colleges & Universities
Cummings for Congress Campaign ♦ Checkers, Inc.

ALLEN PROFESSIONAL GROUP
9900 Cervidas Lane, #3 ▪ Randallstown, MD 21133
410-521-8091

African-American Businesses & Services

CONSULTANTS
Napata Consulting Services ♦ 109 S. Augusta Ave. 644-0142

CONTRACTORS
Allstate Facilities Management, Inc. .... 301-345-4654/474-0145 *(fax)*
   7211 Hanover Parkway, Suite C, Greenbelt, MD
Banks Contracting Company, Inc. 484-1352
Robert Clay, Inc. ♦ 2213 Brookfield Ave. 523-2400
B.A. Harris Construction ♦ 4110 W. Garrison Ave. 367-4175
MD Metro. Assn. of Minority Contractors 523-2400
MD Minority Contractors Assn. ♦ 2530 N. Charles St., Ste. 302 ... 366-5436
P&J Construction ♦ 3010 Ridgewood Ave. 367-2475
Randy Phipps Construction ♦ 6807 Eastridge Rd. 653-6074

ROBERT CLAY CO.
Over 25 Years of Experience

FREE ESTIMATES
QUALITY SERVICE
MHIC# 50653

➥ Licensed
➥ Bonded
➥ Insured

Also Specializes In:

- ➥ Asphalt Paving
- ➥ Bathrooms
- ➥ Church Restoration
- ➥ **Complete Renovation**
- ➥ Concrete
- ➥ Debris Removal
- ➥ Decks
- ➥ Drainage Problems
- ➥ Dr.way Repair
- ➥ Fire Damage
- ➥ Gutters/Downspouts
- ➥ Kitchens
- ➥ Landscaping
- ➥ Patios
- ➥ Retaining Walls
- ➥ **Roofing**
- ➥ Room Additions
- ➥ Rec Rooms
- ➥ **Snow Removal**
- ➥ Vinyl Siding
- ➥ Water Damage
- ➥ Windows/Doors

(301) 953-0474 ➥ (410) 792-0500
Pager: (202) 424-2890 - (410) 478-8530 - Fax: (410) 523-4156
Construction Consultant
Swimming Pool, Patios & Storage

African-American Businesses & Services

Ray Haysbert, Charles Owens, Earl Graves

COPYING SERVICE
Copy Center ♦ 3000 Druid Park Dr., Suite B. 542-5093

COSMETICS
Leslie's Cosmetics 395-9708
Lorne Enterprises 358-0220

CULTURAL PRESENTATIONS
Ancestors Roots, Inc. 664-7632

DANCE
Flair Studio of Dance ♦ 5602 Baltimore National Pike 744-3901
Sanofa Dancers ♦ 4900 Wetheresville Rd. 448-2345

DEBT COUNSELING
Prepare Financial Services ♦ 5406 Reisterstown Rd. 764-0590

DELICATESSEN
Delaney's Cafe ♦ 38 E. 25th Street 243-3400

DELIVERY SERVICE
Daye Delivery Service 740-1343, 800-659-3293

DENTISTS
Adams, Curtis & Cheryl ♦ 2300 Garrison Blvd. 233-3030
Bell, Lawrence ♦ 3326 Auchentroly Terrace 669-0700
Blakely, Maurice ♦ 1519 E. North Ave. 962-1617
Davis, Billy ♦ 4200 Edmondson Ave., Ste. 201 945-8822
Davis, Gladstone ♦ 3701 Liberty Heights Ave. 367-4444
Dental Office ♦ 5418 Park Heights Ave. 542-9000
Desbordes, Fabian ♦ 2300 Garrison Blvd. 362-2910
Hand & Henson ♦ 1826 Woodlawn Dr. 944-8877
Shelton, Benjamin ♦ 1501 E. 33rd St. 243-3714

DERMATOLOGISTS
Gaston, Larry ♦ 2300 Garrison Blvd. 945-7544
Day, Thomas Dr. ♦ 4000 W. Northern Pkwy. 367-7500

Desktop Publishing

Secretary Supreme ♦ 3008 Spaulding Ave. 664-7623
24-Hour Secretary ♦ 1004 Reisterstown Rd., Ste. 200 602-1777
The Perfect Word .... 254-3350/254-7584*(fax)*

The Perfect Word

**PROFESSIONAL OFFICE SUPPORT SERVICE
SPECIALIZING IN SMALL BUSINESSES
OFFICE AUTOMATION & EMPLOYEE TRAINING**

WordProcessing ▪ Network Installation ▪ Office Automation
Computer Consultation ▪ Disaster Recovery ▪ File Management
Proposals ▪ Document Conversion ▪ Bookkeeping

BE A PART OF TODAY'S TECHNOLOGY

Call 410-254-3350 ♦ 410-254-7584 *(fax)*

Disc Jockey

Sugar Chris 408-2179
Old School Productions, Inc./Wedding/Party Specialist 488-2665

Dolls

Baltimore Doll Company ♦ 3711 Pinelea Rd. 655-2483

Domestic Violence

House of Ruth ♦ 2201 Argonne Dr. 889-7884

Dressmakers

Darryl Smith 298-6810

Education

Project Response Learning Center ♦ 2901 Druid Park Dr. 728-6304
Homework, Inc.*(Educational Youth Group)* 354-8805

Electrolysis

Epilation Clinic ♦ 711 W. 40th St., Ste. 208 235-2211

Employment Agencies

Advanced Resource Management ♦ 1900 E. Northern Pkwy, T6... 323-8900
Remedy Personnel ♦ 201 N. Charles St., Ste. 1402 234-8011

Engravers

Thank You Shoppe ♦ 6000 Harford Rd. 426-6222

Entertainment

Bleu Lights Singers 833-7282

African-American Businesses & Services

Entertainment Line ♦ 2114 Park Ave........1800-VIS CITY/327-4266 *(fax)*
Renaissance Productions 728-3837

Entertainment Line, inc.

"Ultimate Resources at Your Fingertips
Baltimore/Washington, D.C. Area

"THINGS TO DO & PLACES TO BE"
(900) 370-2424
First 30 seconds Free!!
Each additional minute just 99¢
(Adult entertainment, must be 18 yrs. or older)

Restaurants - Theaters - Live Entertainment
Tourists Attractions - Nightlife - Shopping Malls
Concerts - Upcoming Events - Sporting Events
Hotels - Radio Stations
For more info. call 1-800-VIS CITY

ESTATE PLANNING
First National Financial Planning.. 647-2523
EXERCISE TRAINERS
Donnacize Aerobic Studio 662-7711
EXPORT
Andecker International 356-7923
EXTERMINATORS
L&S Exterminators... 523-3900
Townes Exterminators.. 323-7825
EYEWEAR
Discount Designer Eyewear ♦ 1532 Havenwood Rd. 467-3157
FAMILY COUNSELING
Ball's Family Therapy ♦ 940 W. Madison Ave., 2nd Fl. 728-7456
Black Mental Health Alliance ♦ 2901 Druid Park Dr. 523-6670
Representative Payee Outreach Center ♦ 163 Wesley Ave. ...800-750-5348
Youth & Families Unlimited Inc. ♦ 6302 Liberty Heights 298-5782

African-American Businesses & Services

> Focusing on Erickson's model of solution oriented brief therapy which builds upon strengths rather than weaknesses

**BALL'S FAMILY THERAPY
IS BRIEF AND SHORT TERM**
Insurance Accepted - Individualized Payments
Sliding Scales - Client Oriented

BALL'S FAMILY THERAPY
940 Madison Avenue ◆ Baltimore, MD
(410) 728-7456 ◆ (410) 435-5135 *(fax)*

Doris L. Ball, LCSW-C - Owner/Operator
Graduate, Morgan St. University and Ohio St. University

FASHION DESIGNERS
Gloria Jennings	367-4935
Lady Sarah's Design & Fashion	764-2805

FINANCIAL PLANNING
Charelene Fonts	547-5011

FLORISTS
Alberta's Florist ◆ 4007 Frederick Ave.	644-6311
Bloomers, Ltd. ◆ 1216 N. Charles St.	752-8850
Bunches of Flowers & Balloons ◆ 37 S. Charles St.	244-1145
Eddie's Flowers ◆ 1277 E. North Ave.	962-5432
Gwynn's Falls Florist ◆ 3300 N. Hilton St.	947-5750
Mallory's Flower Shop ◆ 3108 W. North Ave.	728-1222
Plant Hut ◆ 406 W. Baltimore St.	547-8675

FOOT DOCTOR (Podiatrists)
Mills, Dr. Norris C. ◆ 2200 Garrison Blvd., Ste. 203	945-5400

FORMAL WEAR
Valet Formalwear (2 Locations)
210 Mondawmin Mall	383-1275
1630 McCullouh St.	523-2450

African-American Businesses & Services

FRAMING
Eulipion Art Gallery ◆ 2442 N. Charles St. 235-3922
Expressions Cultural Center ◆ 22 N. Paca St. 783-0195
Family Tree ◆ 825 E. Baltimore St. 576-0880

FRATERNITIES
Alpha Phi Alpha ◆ 2313 St. Paul St. 554-0040
Kappa Alpha Psi ◆ 4903 Liberty Heights Ave. 466-3613
Omega Psi Phi, Inc. ◆ 2003 Presbury St. 462-6705

FUEL OIL
Brice's Oil Company 327-7262
Can Do Fuel Oil Co. ◆ 2527 Baker St. 669-6141
Gladney Oil Company ◆ 2301 Sinclair Lane 522-4900
Murray's Fuel Oil Company ◆ 1318 Bloomingdale Rd. 233-3700

FUNDRAISERS
Black Heritage Products ◆ P.O. Box 3014, 21229 783-5469
Black Heritage Products ❖ Hanover, MD 768-6402

African Heritage Bible

Cost: $46.95

Send credit card information, check or money order, payable to Bible/August Enterprise. 7514 Lemon Tree Ct., Hanover, MD 21076
Name:_____
Address:_____
City/State:_____
Credit Card #:_____
Exp._____Signature:_____
Free Gift with Bible. Phone #:_____

FUNERAL DIRECTORS
Carlton C. Douglass Funeral Service ◆ 1701 McCulloh St. 669-1738
Unity Funeral Home 752-4941

CARLTON C. DOUGLASS FUNERAL SERVICE
THE FINE NAME IN PROFESSIONAL FUNERAL AND EMBALMING SERVICE
Bus. (301) 669-1738
Res. (301) 367-1668
1701 McCULLOH STREET
BALTO. MD. 21217
PAST PRESIDENT
NATIONAL FUNERAL DIRECTORS AND MORTICIANS ASSOCIATION

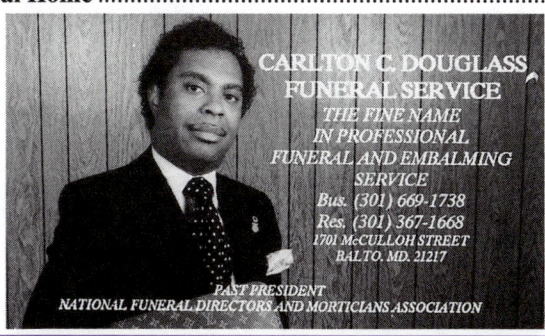

African-American Businesses & Services

FUR SALES & SERVICE
Seleh de Federal Hill Furrier ♦ 1033 S. Charles St. 547-6733

FURNITURE
Ford's Express Co., Inc. ♦ 1420-28 W. Baltimore St. 945-2870
Mattress & More ♦ 2463 Frederick Rd./Westside Shopping Ctr. 945-5675

GENELOGICAL STUDIES
Donna T. Hollie ♦ 2814 Taney Rd. 358-9875

GIFTS SHOPS - *(See Retail Stores)*
Expressions Gift Service 521-9448

GLASS AND MIRROR
Designer Glass & Mirror Co., Inc. ♦ 7429 Harford Rd. 426-2992

GRAPHIC DESIGN
Global Design 581-8913
Jennings Creative Group ♦ 12 W. 25th St. 235-2708

GREETING CARDS/POSTCARDS
Everyone's Place African Cultural Center 728-0877
Heritage Postcard Company ♦ 1937 Druid Hill Ave. 728-8389

HAIR CARE
Kemi Laboratories ♦ 9520 Gerwig Lane, Columbia, MD 381-6664
Shay's Better Braids ♦ 3510 Brenbrook Rd., Randallstown 521-2526

HARDWARE
Saratoga Hardware Store ♦ 109 W. Saratoga St. 752-5786

HATS
Contoured Veilings, Inc. ♦ 401 N. Eutaw St. 727-4539

HEALTH CARE
Liberty Medical Center ♦ 2600 Liberty Heights Ave. 383-4029
Total Health Care (3 Locations)
    1501 Division St. 383-8300
    2149 Kirk Ave. 383-8300
    Mondawmin Mall 669-8800

HERBALIST/IRIDOLOGIST
L & D Herbal Garden 301 449-7438
    7124 Buchanon, Temple Hills, MD

HIV/AIDS SERVICES
HERO ♦ 101 W. Read St. 685-1180
Sisters Together and Reaching, Inc. (S.T.A.R.) 383-1903

HOTELS
Hyatt Regency ♦ 300 Light St. 528-1234
Inn at Pier Five ♦ 711 Eastern Ave. 539-2000
Marriott Inner Harbor ♦ 110 S. Eutaw St. 962-0202

African-American Businesses & Services

INSURANCE

Campbell's Corner ♦ 800 N. Fulton St. 225-3111
McIntyre's Financial & Insurance Services 788-1572
Speaks & Associates 362-6710

462-2639 ▪ 462-2640   462-4981
Bail Bonds   Insurance

*Cody Smith Bail Bond Service, Inc.
Auto Insurance Agency*
Beeper: 281-5566
"WE OFFER IMMEDIATE FREEDOM"

RANDOLPH "CODY" SMITH
Agent/Broker
2409 Reisterstown Rd. ▪ Baltimore, MD 21217

**CAMPBELL BROTHERS
BAIL BOND**
City & County Service
Robert Campbell, Beeper 525-6409
Peggy Campbell, Beeper 525-6574
L. Herrington, Beeper 906-5810
Lela Blue, Beeper 525-7417
Your Kind of Bondsman
410-225-3111/3112
1-800-484-5221 ▪ PIN 311
800 N. Fulton Ave., Baltimore, MD

INFORMATION HOTLINE - 410-783-5469

JANITORIAL/MAINTENANCE SERVICES
Systematic Way, Inc. ♦ 3921 Vero Rd., Ste.A .... 536-0100/536-0102 *(fax)*
Townes Janitorial Service 323-7825

JEWELRY
T.J. Fish Designs ♦ 1219 Greenmount Ave. 539-5630
Yah Ya's Creations 947-3436

LAWN SERVICES
Randall's Lawn Care 323-1860

LEGAL SERVICES
Campbell's & Associates 719-7383
Pre-Paid Legal Services ♦ 4008 Walrad St. 644-8028

LIMOUSINE SERVICE
My Rolls For You, Inc. ♦ 3700 Frankford Ave. 254-8058
Paramount Limousine Service ♦ 2000 Aisquith St. 889-3100
Scruggs Enterprises ♦ 1412 E. Preston St. 685-0871

LIQUOR STORES
Harbor Liquors ♦ 10 E. Lombard St. 547-1446
Mid-Town Spirit & Wine Cellar ♦ 17 W. Biddle St. 539-4873
Plaza Liquor ♦ 5722 Wabash Ave. 358-8045

MAGAZINES
Buzz-n' Round Baltimore 323-7001
Charm City Connector ♦ P.O Box 3014, 21229 783-5469

African-American Businesses & Services

Minority MBA ♦ 3610 Sequoia Ave. 367-2710
Power Magazine *(Christian Information NewsCalendar)* 653-9501
Sister Shout 683-3415

MAGICIANS
William H. Gross ♦ 1417 Gitting Ave .... 323-5189/796-6805 *(pager)*

MARKETING
G.F.E. Marketing ♦ 5430 Old Court Rd., Randallstown 521-5629
Mid-Atlantic Marketing Consultants ♦ 1816 N. Charles St. 752-6460
Pro-Baltimore ♦ 1322 Eutaw St., Ste. 2R .... 462-1285/462-3529 *(fax)*
Umoja Sasa Prevention Marketing Group 576-8688

MASSAGE THERAPY
Arlinda's Place ♦ 2076 Lord Baltimore Dr. 298-8778
Motion by Mildred 391-4602

MODELING TROUPE
Flair Modeling Agency ♦ 5602 Baltimore National Pike 744-3901
Travis Winkey ♦ 2515 Liberty Heights Ave. 225-7755

MOVING COMPANIES
Ford's Express Co., Inc. ♦ 1420-28 W. Baltimore St. 945-2870
Thomas Moving & Hauling ♦ 1823 Pennsylvania Ave. 728-1655
Williams Moving & Distribution Company ♦ 9707 Winands Rd. . 521-1057

MORTGAGE CONSULTANT

Carl Suber, Mortgage Consultant

INTEREST RATES HAVE
FALLEN

Free Mortgage Consultation

"***Do you want to take advantage of the strong mortgage market?*** Let **Carl Suber** be your mortgage consultant. With almost a decade in the mortgage industry Carl has helped people searching for the ***best rates*** in town as well as those with less than perfect credit ***save hundreds of dollars*** each month.

G S F MORTGAGE CORPORATION CAN HELP YOU . . .
*Purchase a home *Refinance an exisiting mortgage *Consolidate Your Loans *Make Home Improvements & Repairs *Obtain the Rates and Terms to Suit your Individual Needs *Save Money Every Month Through Consolidation and Low Interest Rates!

301-953-3817 • 410-880-4895 (Baltimore) **• 1-800-454-8492** *Pager*

African-American Businesses & Services

MUSIC STORES

Dimensions in Music ♦ 221 & 229 N. Charles St. 752-1121
Rome Records ♦ 2423 Frederick Ave. (Westside Shopping Center) 947-2676
Scooter G International Records ♦ 1904 Charles St. 752-1207

Music is Our Beat!

SCOOTER "G" INTERNATIONAL RECORD SHOP

1904 North Charles St. ♦ Baltimore, Maryland 21218

410-752-1207

CD's
Cassette Tapes
Record Cleaners
Stereo Accessories

R & B Records
Jazz
Soca
Regga
Gospel

American Pop
Rap
Video Tapes

LADIES AND MEN'S FASHION ACCESSORIES

You Need It, We Will Get It!

BALTIMORE - WHERE BLACK HERITAGE BEGINS

Musicians

Lionel Jiggetts	947-9442
Graffiti Jazz	408-4494

Nail Salons

Glory of Kedar, Inc. ♦ 210 W. Fayette St.	244-6245
Nail Y Mas ♦ 150 S. Collins Ave.	646-4613

Nail Y Mas
Nail Salon

Manicures - Nail Designs - Nail Tips & Wraps
Sculptured Nails - Pedicures
150 S. Collins Ave., Baltimore, MD

Beatrice Gaston

410- 646-4613

Newspapers

Baltimore Times ♦ 12 W. 25th St.	366-3900
Afro-American Newspaper ♦ 2509 N. Charles St.	554-8200
La Rave Fashions News ♦ 2414 Liberty Hgts Ave.	225-7102
Minority Business Enterprise ♦ 4806 Seton Dr., Ste. 3	764-0040

Nightclubs

Arch Social Club ♦ 2426 Pennsylvania Ave.	669-9856
Alpha House (APA)	554-0040
Blue Caribbean, ♦ 542 Park Heights Ave.	664-1550
Caton Castle ♦ Caton Ave. & Hilton St.	566-7086
Choices ♦ 1817 N. Charles St.	752-4602
Eldorado Gentlemen Lounge ♦ Baltimore St.	727-1509
Elks Monumental Lodge #3 ♦ 528 Madison St.	383-0826
Five Mile House ♦ 5302 Reisterstown Rd.	542-4895
Haven Lounge ♦ 1532 Argonne Dr., (Northwood Shopping Ctr)	366-7416
Kappa Alpha Psi House ♦ 4903 Liberty Heights Ave.	367-9520
Louie Louie's ♦ 1101 S. Howard St.	727-2005
Mariah's ♦ 540 Winters Lane	788-0700
Omega Psi Phi House ♦ 2003 Presbury St.	462-6705
Ritz East ♦ 5500 Sinclair Lane	483-5555

African-American Businesses & Services

Roots Bar & Lounge ♦ 2148 Vine Street 945-7398
Silver Shadow ♦ K & M Lakefront North, Columbia, MD 730-0111
Sportsman Lounge ♦ 4723 Gwynn Oak Ave. 664-1041
Tony's Place ♦ 3801 Old York Rd. 366-4817
Vulcan Blazers ♦ 2811 Druid Park Dr. 367-4157
Wall St. Lounge ♦ 1818 Maryland Ave. 625-3873
Whitten's Lounge ♦ 5430 Sinclair Lane 325-7572

NOTARY PUBLIC
Alagra McClendon 233-7275
The Perfect Word .... 254-3350/254-7584*(fax)*

NURSE
Black Nurses Association .... P.O. Box 6975 21216

NUTRITION
Healthy Choices ♦ 130 W. 25th St. 467-0506

OFFICE SUPPLIES
Sue-Ann's Office Supply ♦ 4137 Patterson Ave. 358-5837
Qualls Office Supplies ♦ 2901 Druid Park Dr. 225-3775

OPTICIANS
Ashburton Opticians ♦ 3020 Liberty Heights Ave. 664-9446
A&J Opticians 000-0000
Discount Designer Eyewear ♦ 1532 Havenwood Rd. 467-3152
R. Wright Optical ♦ 5335 Reisterstown Rd. 358-0954

OPHTHALMOLOGY
Schmoke, Dr. Patricia ♦ 2600 Liberty Heights 578-1515

PAGING COMPANY
The Pager Store ♦ 4119 Patterson Ave. 764-5678

PAINT DISTRIBUTOR
Any Color Paint Company ♦ 5114 Liberty Heights Ave. 466-7278

PARTY PLANNERS
Allen Professional Service 521-8091
Special Touches by Pamela ♦ 542 Chateau Ave. 433-2389

PHYSICAL THERAPY
Burs & Garrett ♦ 2530 N. Charles St. 889-7872

PHOTOGRAPHERS
J.D. Howard 486-7997
Frederick Monroe 728-8389
John Murphy, III 367-4292
Glasco Royales ♦ 226 Park Ave. 659-9365

PODIATRIST
C. Norris Mills, D.P.M. & Associates ♦ 2200 Garrison Blvd. 945-5400

African-American Businesses & Services

PRESENTATIONS
Ideas & Images 435-5004
The Perfect Word .... 254-3350/254-7584*(fax)*

PRINTING
Harvest Printing & Graphics♦ .... 301-596-7553/410-381-1833 *(fax)*
 9689-E Gerwig Lane, Columbia, MD
Mack Printing ♦ 910 Poplar Grove St. 945-3441
Time Printing ♦ 227 N. Warwick 566-3005
Wells Printer ♦ 1112 N. Fremont St. 728-6618
Specialty Marketing & Printing ♦ 9008 Liberty Rd. 922-1233
The Power 653-9501

PUBLISHING
Black Classic Press ♦ P.O. Box 13414 358-0980
Duncan & Duncan ♦ P.O. Box 1137, Edgewood, MD 538-5579
Melchizedek Priesthood Publishing Association 433-0811

RADIO STATIONS
Radio One♦ 100 St. Paul St. 481-1010
 WOLB 1010 AM ♦ Magic 95.9 FM ♦ **92Q** 92.3 FM ♦ WWIN 1400 AM
WEAA 88.9 FM ♦ Morgan State University 319-3564
WBGR 860 AM ♦ 300 Druid Park Dr. 367-7773
V103 - 103.2 FM ♦ Heaven 600 AM 653-2200

REAL ESTATE APPRAISALS
W.A. Barkley, C.G.A. ♦ 800 N. Bentalou St. 362-65700
Webb and Webb Realty, Inc. 358-7379

RECREATION CENTER
Rognel Heights Recreation Center ♦ 1200 Wicklow Rd. 396-0160

RESTAURANTS/EATERIES/CARRYOUT
Braznel Caribbean Kitchen ♦ 1623 E. Baltimore St. 327-2445
Cafe Pangeo ♦ 4007 Falls Rd. 662-0500
Class Act Catering & Cafe ♦ 628 N. Chester St. 728-8880
Delaney's Deli ♦ 38 E. 25th St. 243-3400
Five Mile House ♦ 5302 Reisterstown Rd. 542-4895
Haven Lounge ♦ 1532 Argonne Dr. (Northwood Shopping Ctr) 366-7416
Lake Trout Carry-out .... Reisterstown Rd. & Haywood St.
Larry Stewart's Place ♦ 21 S. Calvert Street 752-5715
La Tesso Tana ♦ 58 W. Biddle St. 837-3630
Mariah's Restaurant ♦ 540 Winters Lane 788-0700
Micah's Restaurant ♦ 5401 Reisterstown Rd. 764-7240/9206
Redwood Grill ♦ 12 S. Calvert St. 244-8550

African-American Businesses & Services

RETAIL SHOPS

(d) *denotes Downtown*

African-American Fashions ◆ 7031 Liberty Rd. 281-1310
African Fashions & Cultural Store ◆ 3816 Liberty Heights Ave. ... 664-5141
Afrocentric Unique Boutique ◆ 2711A Hanson Ave. 764-7186
Bible Store ◆ 17 N. Eutaw St. (d) 539-2847
Boutique Unlimited ◆ 5421 York Rd. 323-7727
Delana Fashions ◆ 622 N. Eutaw St. (d) 728-0446
Expressions Cultural Center ◆ 222 N. Paca St. (d) 783-0195
Everyone's Place ◆ 1356 W. North Ave. 728-0877
Fisher's Neckties & Accessories ◆ 419 N. Eutaw St. (d) 727-7446
Greg's Fashions II ◆ 3129 W. North Ave. 566-9144
Handbags - It's In The Bag ◆ 3119 Mayfair Rd. 298-4673
Harris Enterprise ◆ 4003 Sanlee Rd., Randallstown 655-2913
Just For Fun Boutique ◆ 34 Market Place (d) 752-6838
Maggie's Place ◆ 213 Read St. (d) 728-5678
My Special Place ◆ 128 W. North Ave. 685-3434
Out of Africa ◆ 111 W. Saratoga St. (d) 752-5808
Repetez Nearly New Shop ◆ 4724 Liberty Heights Ave. 542-6222
Rhonda's Boutique ◆ 1817 Whitehead 594-1881
Rucker's & Company ◆ 319 W. Franklin St.(d) 539-5010
Sankofa African Enterprises ◆ 2116 N. Charles St. 685-5774
Shoe Salon, The ◆ 9834 Liberty Rd., Randallstown 655-5644
Sibanye ◆ 4031 W. Rogers Ave. 358-5806

SEAFOOD
Tommy's Seafood ◆ 2101 E. Monument St., 21205 *(N.E. Market)* 563-0340

SECRETARIAL SERVICE
The Perfect Word .... 254-3350/254-7584 *(fax)*
24-Hour Secretary ◆ 1004 Reisterstown Rd., Ste. 200 602-1777

SECURITY SERVICE
Watkins Security Agency ◆ 116 Metro Plaza 523-5080

SERVICE STATIONS
AMOCO .... Lafayette & Monroe
         North & McCullough ◆ Liberty Hgts & Gwynn Oak ◆ Gwynn Falls

SHIRTS
Quality Tailoring ◆ 5 Light St. 685-6411
Shirtery ◆ 2901 Druid Park Dr. 669-2726

SHOES
Tyese ◆ 2439 St. Paul St. 662-7442

African-American Businesses & Services

SHOE REPAIR
Happy Feet ✦ 5668 The Alameda *(Belvedere Plaza)* 435-FEET
Malcolm's Shoe Repair ✦ 2100 W. Fayette St. 945-9884

SIGNS
KO-N Village Signs ✦ 2430 St. Paul St. 243-5324
Washington Signs ✦ 3200 Loch Raven Boulevard 243-3279

SORORITIES
Delta Sigma Theta, Inc. 521-9378

SPORTS APPAREL
Foot Stop ✦ 4574 Edmondson Ave .... 947-7644/947-7646*(fax)*
M & E Sports ✦ 3810 Cedar Dr. .... 944-8056 ✦ 800-397-5464
Negro League Baseball Collectibles 783-5469
Simmons Sportswear ✦ 2107½ Gwynn Oak Ave. 298-4034

TAILORS
Quality Tailoring, Inc. ✦ 5 Light St. 685-6414

TAX SERVICES
Bert, Bell & Bounds ✦ 5201 Reisterstown Rd. 466-6000

TEE-SHIRT/SCREEN PRINTERS
B.C. Teez ✦ 4946 Clifton Ave. 448-5907
Bustertizin' ✦ 235 N. Franklintown Rd. 233-0198
Harvest Printing & Graphics .... 410-596-7553/381-1838*(fax)*
   9689-E Gerwig Lane ✦ Columbia, MD

TELEVISION SHOW
ABN Cable TV 542-0411
The Dream Network 301-565-5948
That Show With Those Black Guys 381-4775

THEATERS
Arena Players ✦ 801 McCullough St. 728-6500
Encore Theatre ✦ 4801 Liberty Heights Ave. 466-2433
Heritage Cinema Playhouse ✦ 12 E. 25th Street 764-0320
Tower Theatre ✦ 6301 Reisterstown Rd. 358-1131

TOURS
Baltimore Black Heritage Tours ✦ *Louis Fields* 783-5469
Black Landmarks Tours ✦ *Tom Saunders* 728-3837
SiteSeeing Tours, Inc. ❖ Silver Spring, MD... 301-445-2098/445-3821*(fax)*

TOWING
Half-Price Towing .... 655-6352/471-7302*(pager)*

TRAVEL AGENT
Adventures In Travel ✦ 3900 N. Charles St. ...... 467-1161/467-1159*(fax)*
All About You Travel 323-2428
Avant Garde Travel, Ltd. 987-0033/578-9327

African-American Businesses & Services

Campbell & Associates, For reservations call 800-873-5353 pin #0221479 719-7383
DCM Travel 662-1797
Lotus Travel Services Agency ✦ 1111 Park Ave., Ste. 5B 669-3104
Mondawmin Travel ✦ Mondawmin Mall 669-8200
Rooks & Co. Travel Service ✦ 1917 Park Ave., Ste. 200 528-1188
Ultimate Travel Network ✦ 2539 St. Paul St., #A.... 889-6297/889-6298*(fax)*

UPHOLSTERING
Cherry's Upholstering Company ✦ 4805 Garrison Blvd................. 664-3364
Steven Pace Upholstery Company ✦ 729 Frederick Rd.................. 744-0640

Phone: 664-3364   Est. 1939

CHERRY'S UPHOLSTERING CO.
The Work We Do Speaks For Us

JAMES CHERRY Jr.   *Vinyl Covers*
Sales Manager   *Made To Order*

UTILITIES AUDITOR
Collins & Associates ✦ 4 W. Bend Ct............................847-5688 or 281-1269

VARIETY STORES
D'Lynns ✦ 3828 W. Forest Park St. 367-2405
Good & Cheap ✦ 5220 Park Heights Ave. 578-3815

VIDEO SERVICE
Renae Johnson.. 358-6906
SideShow Productions ✦ 4806 Seton Dr., Ste. 207 764-0065

WHOLESALERS
D & E Photography & Fashions ✦ 1907 Woodlawn Dr. 298-6262
Nappy Collectibles ✦ P.O. Box 20933, 20923.................................. 602-3477

WINDOW COVERINGS
J & B Glover Window Coverings 254-8286

WINDOW TINTING
Quality Window Tinting ✦ 5327 Liberty Heights Ave...................... 664-0219

YOUTH TRAINING
Homework, Inc. 354-8805
Woodstock Job Corps Center 461-1100

TRAVEL GUIDE

MARYLAND TOURISM OFFICES

ALLEGANY COUNTY (ALL)
301-777-5905 or 800-50-VISIT
301-759-1329 (fax)

ANNE ARUNDEL COUNTY & ANNAPOLIS
(AAR) 410-280-0445/410-263-9591 (fax)

BALTIMORE CITY
410-837-4636
800-282-6632/410-727-6769 (fax)

BALTIMORE COUNTY (BCO)
410-583-7313 or 800-570-2836
410-583-7327 (fax)

CALVERT COUNTY (CAL)
410-535-4583 - 410-535-1787(fax)
301-855-1880(DC) - 800-331-9771

CAROLINE COUNTY (CRN)
410-479-4188/410-479-4200 (fax)
410-479-3625

CARROLL COUNTY (CAR)
410-857-2983 or 800-272-1933
410-876-1560 (fax)

CECIL COUNTY (CEC)
410-996-5300 or 800-CECIL-95

CHARLES COUNTY (CHR)
301-934-9305 - 301-870-3388(DC)
800-766-3386/301-934-5624 (fax)

DORCHESTER COUNTY (DOR)
800-522-TOUR or 410-228-1000
410-228-6848 (fax)

FREDERICK COUNTY (FRE)
301-663-8687 or 800-999-3613
301-663-0039 (fax)

GARRETT COUNTY (GAR)
310-334-1948/301-334-1919 (fax)

HARFORD COUNTY (HAR)
410-879-2000 x. 339 (Balto. line)
410-638-3339 or 410-597-2649
410-879-8043 (fax)

HOWARD COUNTY (HOW)
410-313-1900 or 800-288-TRIP
410-313-1902 (fax)

KENT COUNTY (KEN)
410-778-0416 (same fax #)

MONTGOMERY COUNTY (MON)
301-428-9702 or 800-925-0880
301-428-9705 (fax)

PRINCE GEORGE'S COUNTY (PRG)
301-925-8300/301-925-2053 (fax)

QUEEN ANNE'S COUNTY (QUA)
410-827-4810/410-827-4947 (fax)

ST. MARY's COUNTY (STM)
301-475-1626 - 301-475-4105 (TDD)
800-327-9023/301-475-4414 (fax)

SOMERSET COUNTY (SOM)
410-651-2968 or 800-521-9189
410-651-3917 (fax)

TALBOT COUNTY (TAL)
410-882-4606/410-822-7922 (fax)

WASHINGTON COUNTY (WAS)
301-791-3246 or 800-228-STAY
301-791-3175 (VOICE/TTY)
301-791-2601 (fax)

WICOMICO COUNTY (WIC)
410-548-4914 or 800-332-TOUR
410-548-4917 (fax)

WORCESTER COUNTY & OCEAN CITY
410-632-3617/410-632-2141 (fax)

OCEAN CITY CONVENTION &
VISITORS BUREAU
410-289-8181/410-289-0058 (fax)

TOWN OF OCEAN CITY
410-289-2800/410-289-0058 (fax)

Robert Steele
General Manager

The Most Accommodating Place On The Harbor.

The **Hyatt Regency Baltimore** is the gateway to the Inner Harbor. Whether you're in for a meeting, a weekend getaway, dining and dancing, or just a relaxing Sunday brunch, come discover the people with the *Hyatt Touch*.

For more information call (410) 528-1234.

It all starts right here.

HYATT REGENCY BALTIMORE
ON THE INNER HARBOR

Louis C. Fields, Patrick Fragale-, Lester Lockett - Negro Leagues Baseball Player

The Best in Service, Location and Value

With over 500 rooms, including 35 suites, 14,000 square feet of meeting space. The Marriott's Grand Ballroom can accommodate up to 1,000 guests.

Conveniently located near The Inner Harbor Attractions:

The Downtown Business District, Oriole Park at Camden Yard, The Baltimore Convention Center, and Lexington Market are all within a short walking distance of the Marriott.

BALTIMORE Marriott

INNER HARBOR HOTEL

110 South Eutaw Street • Baltimore, Maryland 21201 • (410) 962-0202

BALTIMORE - WHERE BLACK HERITAGE BEGINS - 120

BALTIMORE CITY ATTRACTIONS

Use 410 area code

American Visionary Art Museum .... 800 Key Highway ☎ 244-1900
Original works of art created by intuitive, self-taught artists.

Antique Row .... 841 N. Howard Street ☎ 675-4776

Babe Ruth Birthplace & Baseball Center .... ☎ 727-1539
216 Emory Street - Exhibits on Babe Ruth, the Baltimore Orioles, and Maryland baseball.

Baltimore Arena .... 201 W. Baltimore Street ☎ 347-2020
Sports and entertainment center.

Baltimore Convention Center .... 1 W. Pratt Street ☎ 659-7000
The Center has increased available exhibit space to over 300,000 sq.ft. and meeting space to 87,000 sq.ft.

Baltimore American Indian Center ...... 113 S. Broadway ☎ 675-3535
The Center houses a museum and offers cultural workshops.

Baltimore City Hall .... 100 N. Holliday ☎ 396-4900

Baltimore City Life Museums ...... 800 E. Lombard Street ☎ 396-3523
➢ Carroll Mansion - Restored home of the Marylander who was a signer of the Declaration of Independence, Charles Carroll.
➢ Center for Archaeology-Exhibition features 18th & 19th century artifacts, life-sized excavation pit and working lab.
➢ 1840 House - Living history museum takes visitors to 19th century Baltimore through drama and "hands-on" programs.
➢ Courtyard Exhibition Center - rotating exhibits on city living themes.
➢ Morton Blaustein Exhibitor Hall

LIVING AND WORKING AND WORSHIPING AND PLAYING AND STRUGGLING ...

Baltimore **CityLife** Museums *We're telling your story.*

Make your first stop in Baltimore our new Morton K. Blaustein City Life Exhibition Center
opening April 12, 1996. • 33 S. Front St. • (410) 396-3523

QUESTION: Charles L. Reason, George B. Vashon and James Madison Bell all wrote poetry for what cause?

◄ **BLACK FACT** ►

Answer: The abolition of slavery.

BALTIMORE - WHERE BLACK HERITAGE BEGINS

Baltimore City Attractions

Baltimore Museum of Art.................. Charles St. at 31st ☎ 396-7101
Maryland's largest art museum, featured art from Africa, America, Asia and Oceana.

Baltimore Museum of Industry.......... 1415 Key Highway ☎ 727-4808
Chronicles Baltimore's industrial and labor history. Exhibits include a 19th century print shop, garment loft and the 1906 steam tugboat Baltimore.

Baltimore Public Works Museum .... 751 Eastern Ave. ☎ 396-5565
Housed in a historic pumping station, exhibits and media presentations on public works history and urban environmental history of Baltimore.

Baltimore Streetcar Museum................. 1901 Falls Road ☎ 547-0264
History of streetcars of Baltimore.

Basilica of the National Shrine of The Assumption of the Blessed Virgin Mary .... Cathedral & Mulberry Streets ☎ 727-3564
The first Catholic Cathedral in the U.S. Designed by Benjamin Latrobe, architect of U.S. Capitol.

B&O Railroad Museum .... 901 W. Pratt St. ☎ 752-2490
Site of first American railroad terminal and one of the world's finest collections of railroading artifacts and memorabilia.

Camden Station .... 333 W. Camden Street
First railroad station in the U.S.

CenterStage .... 700 N. Calvert Street ☎ 332-0033
The State Theater of Maryland presents exciting theatrical productions.

Columbus Center .... Pier 3, Inner Harbor ☎ 576-5700
A maritime center.

Cylburn Arboretum..................... 4915 Greenspring Ave. ☎ 396-0180
The 176 acre estate features gardens, trails and a hands-on museum and library.

Edgar Allen Poe House..................... 203 N. Amity Street ☎ 396-7932
This house is where Poe began his writing career.

Enoch Pratt Free Library .... Central Branch ☎ 396-5430
400 Cathedral Ave.

Baltimore City Attractions

Fells Point .... Broadway & Fleet Sts. ☎ 675-4776
Located on the waterfront, dating back to 1730, features many boutiques, dining, walking tours, antiques, local pubs; once was home to Frederick Douglass.

Fire Museum of Maryland .... 1301 York Road ☎ 321-7500
Built in 1799, one of the oldest fire stations, memorabilia, and photographs.

Flag House & 1812 Museum .... 844 E. Pratt Street. ☎ 837-1793
Built in 1793, original home of Mary Pickersgill, maker of the flag that flew over Ft. McHenry during the War of 1812 and inspired Francis Scott Key to write the National Anthem.

Fort McHenry National Monument & Historic Shrine ... ☎ 962-4290
Fort Avenue; The successful defense of this star shaped brick fort occurred on September 13, 1814. Exhibits include guardrooms, officers' quarters and barracks.

HarborPlace/The Gallery .... Pratt & Light Sts. ☎ 332-4191
Maryland's premier tourist attraction featuring retail shops and eateries, encircled by Baltimore's top tourist attractions.

H.L. Mencken House .... 1524 Hollins Street
Former home of writer Henry Louis Mencken known as the Sage of Baltimore.

Holocaust Memorial & Sculpture .... Water, Gay & Lombard Sts.
Erected in 1980, a memorial to the Jewish people murdered by the Nazis in Europe between 1933-1945.

Homewood House Museum .... ☎ 515-5589
Johns Hopkins Univ. Campus (3400 N. Charles Street) 19th Century home of Charles Carroll, Jr.

Jewish Historical Society of Maryland .... ☎ 321-7500

Jewish Heritage Center .... 15 Lloyd Street ☎ 732-6400
Includes a museum, library, archives, collections and two restored historic synagogues. The country's largest institution devoted to regional American Jewish history.

Lacrosse Hall of Fame .... 113 W. University Pkwy. ☎ 235-6882
A national museum of America's first sport, showcases 350 years of lacrosse's greatest moments.

Baltimore City Attractions

Lexington Market..............................300 N. Eutaw Street ☎ 685-6169
Various ethnic/American eateries and retail shops.

Lovely Lane United Methodist Church & Museum .... ☎ 889-1512
2200 St. Paul St.-Mother church of American Methodist (1772)

Market Center .. bounded by Franklin, Liberty, Baltimore & Greene St. Over 400 merchants with discount stores, ethnic foods and specialty shops and Lexington Market.

Maryland Historical Society ....210 W. Monument Street ☎ 685-3750
C.1844-An independent museum/library of Maryland history. Home of original "Star Spangled Banner" manuscript.

Maryland Institute, College of Art.....................................☎ 669-9200
1300 Mount Royal Ave. - The nation's oldest independent college of art features works by students and faculty.

Maryland Science Center........................601 Light Street ☎ 685-5225
Imax Theater and Davis Planetarium.

Mother Seton House ....600 N. Paca Street ☎ 523-3443
In honor of the first American-born canonized saint.

Mount Claire Museum House.....1500 Washington Blvd. ☎ 837-3262
C.1760-Baltimore's only pre-revolutionary war mansion.

EXPLORE YOUR HISTORY
AT THE MARYLAND HISTORICAL SOCIETY

Joshua Johnson Collection
A collection of paintings by the first African-American professional painter.

Mining The Museum
A work of installation art by artist Fred Wilson, who used the society's collections to explore the African-American and Native American experiences in Maryland.

Eubie Blake, 1883-1983
A display of the memorabilia of the great musician and Baltimore native described by President Ronald Reagan as "a pioneer crusader for black Americans in the world of art and entertainment."

Maryland Historical Society
201 West Monument Street
in the historic Mount Vernon neighborhood
410-685-3750

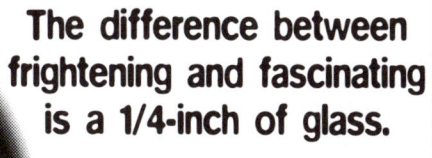

The difference between frightening and fascinating is a 1/4-inch of glass.

Come see some of the most unusual creatures the way you've always wanted to see them. Behind glass. Jellies: Phantoms of the Deep. The mysterious new exhibit at the National Aquarium in Baltimore.

NATIONAL AQUARIUM IN BALTIMORE

Call 410-576-3800 for more information.

1896-1979 — Henry Hall

Henry Hall was an African American who donated his rare fish collection to the National Aquarium in Baltimore even before it was built. Hall, sometimes called the "Father of Baltimore's Black Engineers," donated his freshwater fish collection to the Aquarium in 1977, two years before his death. Hall was interested in fish from the time he was a very small child. He used to get his mother's pots and pans and catch frogs and tadpoles with them. As an adult, Hall's interest in fish and aquariums grew. He built an "Elaborate" aquarium that filled almost the whole of his basement at his Mosher Street home. He also made the tanks and filters that housed his collection. The $10,000 collection included 35 rare and outstanding species such as electric eels, an alligator, carp, an albino walking catfish (a species that may no longer be imported into this country), snake eaters, a large red-tailed catfish, lungfish, oscars, clown knifefish and a shovelnose catfish, to name some. After the fish were moved from Hall's home, they were housed at the Maryland Academy of Sciences where they remained until they were taken to Pier 3 for public display.

Baltimore City Attractions

Nine North Front Street.......................... 9 N. Front Street ☎ 837-5424
C. 1790 home of the second mayor of Baltimore. Current headquarters of The Women's City League.

Oriole Park at Camden Yards...........333 W. Camden St. ☎ 685-9800

Otterbein United Methodist Church .... ☎ 685-4703
Sharp & Conway Streets. Oldest church in continuous use in Baltimore, built in 1785.

Peabody Conservatory of Music...................................... ☎ 659-8165
One E. Mt Vernon Place. The oldest music school in the U.S.

Peale Museum..225 Holliday St. ☎ 396-3523
Baltimore oldest museum (1814). Served as Baltimore's first City Hall and is the oldest building in the western hemisphere, specially designed to house a museum.

Pimlico Race Track .... Hayward & Park Heights Ave. ☎ 542-9400
Home of the Preakness Stakes, 3rd Saturday in May.

Pride of Baltimore II .... Inner Harbor
The only existing replica of a 1812 era Baltimore Clipper topsail schooner.

Shot Tower...Front & Fayette Street
Interactive exhibits and a sight, sound and light show illustrate the story of how gun shot was made in this 215 foot structure.

St. Jude Shrine ....Paca &Saratoga Sts. ☎ 685-6026

St. Vincent de Paul Church .... 120 N. Front Street ☎ 862-5078
Baltimore's oldest Catholic Church.

Star-Spangled Banner Flag House &
1812 Museum ....844 E. Pratt St. ☎ 837-1793

Top Of The World ...World Trade Center, 410 E. Pratt St. ☎ 837-4515
Top floor offers grand view of Baltimore.

U.S. Constellation............................. Pier 1 Inner Harbor ☎ 539-1797

Walters Art Gallery ....600 N. Charles St. ☎ 547-9000
22,000 works of art including Ethopian, American, Asian, etc.

War Memorial Building & Plaza..... Lexington & Gay Sts. ☎ 685-7530
Honors American soldiers and citizens

Washington Monument............................ Charles at Mt. Vernon Place
178 foot statue, U.S. first monument honoring George Washington.

BIBLIOGRAPHY

Asante, Dr. Molefi Kete. African American History. People's Publishing Group, 1995

Baltimore African American Heritage Visitor's Guide, Baltimore Office of Promotion

Diggs, Louis, It All Started On Winters Lane. 1995

Ebony Editors. Ebony Pictorial History of Black America. Southwestern Co.

Franklin & Moss. From Slavery to Freedom. McGraw-Hill, 1987

Gourse, Leslie. Dizzy Gillespie & The Birth of BeBop. Atheneum, 1994

Gutman, Herbert G. The Black Family In Slavery And Freedom. Vintage Books, 1976

Harris, Levitt, Furman, Smith. The Black Book. Random House

Kliment, Bud. Billie Holiday. Chelsea House Publishers, 1990

Koger, A. Briscoe. Negro Baptists of Maryland

Mannix, Daniel P. Black Cargoes, A History of The Atlantic Slave Trade. The Viking Press, 1962

Medearis, Angela S. The Seven Days of Kwanzaa. Scholastic Inc. 1994

Riley, James A. The Biographical Encyclopedia of the Negro Leagues. Carroll & Graf Publishers, 1994

Riley, James A. Dandy, Day, & Devil. TK Publishers, 1987.

Katz, William L. Eyewitness: The Negro In American History.

Salley, Columbus. The Black 100. Citadel Press Book. 1993

PHOTO CREDITS

J.D. HOWARD - Front Cover, pgs. 2, 4, 6, 8-9, 12, 16, 24, 28, 29, 31, 86-87, 89; L.C. FIELDS - pgs. 5, 21, 54, 56, 58, 110; RAY GILBERT, pg. 120; J.M. JOHNSON - pg. 53; FREDERICK MONROE - pg. 34, 76; DICK MYERS - pg. 63; OWENS - pg. 63; RICK ROBINSON - pg. 59, 61, 103; SILBER PHOTOGRAPHY - pg. 3 VICKY SPALDING - pg. 46; TONY WHITE - pg. 17

Lift Every Voice and Sing

Lift every voice and sing till earth and heaven ring
Ring with the harmonies of liberty;
Let our rejoicing rise high as the listening skies,
Let it resound loud as the rolling sea.
Sing a song full of the faith that the dark past has taught us,
Sing a song full of the hope that the present has brought us.
Facing the rising sun of our new day begun
Let us march on til victory is won.

Stony the road we trod, bitter the chastening rod
Felt in the days when hope unborn had died;
Yet with a steady beat have not our weary feet
Come to the place for which our fathers sighed.
We have come over the way that with tears has been watered
We have come treading our path through the blood of the slaughtered-
Out of the gloomy past, till now we stand at last
Where the white gleam of our bright star is cast.

God of our weary years, God of our silent tears,
Thou who has brought us far on our way,
Thou who has by Thy might led us into the light
Keep us forever in Thy path we pray.
Lest our feet stray from the places our God where we met Thee,
Lest our hearts, drunk with the wine of the world, we forget Thee,
Shadowed beneath Thy hand may we forever stand
True to our God, true to our native land.

by James Weldon Johnson

Original Photo of Million Man March

Copyright 1995 by J.D. Howard

To order copies call 410-486-7999

Battle Reenactment at Antietam, Washington County. Baseball at Oriole Park at Camden Yards.

So many things to do. So close together.

MARYLAND

Call for a free travel kit or call your travel agent.
1·800·266·5699

ISBN# 0-9655741-0-5